PORTFOLIO
DESIGN

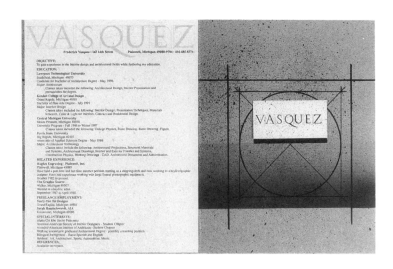

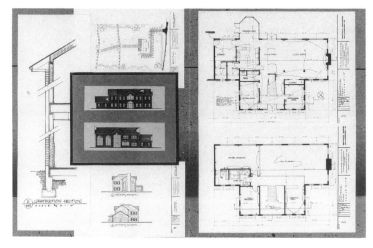

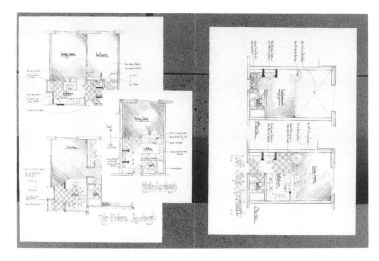

PORTFOLIO
DESIGN

THIRD EDITION

Harold Linton

Photographs by Steven Rost

W. W. Norton & Company

New York • London

For information about permission to reproduce
selections from this book, write to Permissions,
W. W. Norton & Company, Inc., 500 Fifth Avenue,
New York, NY 10110

Manufacturing by Edwards Brothers
Book design by Charlotte Staub
Production by Ken Gross
Production Manager: Leeann Graham

Library of Congress Cataloging-in-Publication Data

Linton, Harold
    Portfolio design / Harold Linton; photographs by
Steven Rost. —3rd ed.
        p.   cm.
    Includes bibliographical references and index.
    ISBN 0-393-73095-6
    1. Architecture portfolios—Design. 2. Architectural
services marketing. 3. Design services—Marketing.
I. Rost, Steven. II. Title.

NA1996.L56   2003
720'.23—dc21   2003046489

W. W. Norton & Company, Inc., 500 Fifth Avenue,
New York, N.Y. 10110
www.wwnorton.com

W. W. Norton & Company Ltd., Castle House, 75/76
Wells St., London W1T 3QT

0 9 8 7 6 5 4

To my wife, Deeni, for matching rockers.

CONTENTS

Among the many ingredients that help define an excellent portfolio, coherence and modesty are paramount. Plain is better than fancy; simple much better than complicated. The portfolio is a tool for conveying a sense of the work; it should not be an advertisement for itself.

Robert A. M. Stern
School of Architecture
Yale University

FOREWORD

When I look at a design portfolio, I am interested in the content, of course; but I am
also interested in the design of the portfolio
itself. Sometimes it tells me as much as the
work it presents. In it, I can judge the person's
eye: the images chosen, how they are placed
on a page, how the captions are designed, the
choice of type, the color of paper, the design
of the cover. I can also tell if the designer is
conservative, adventuresome, flashy, restrained, neat, or sloppy.

The portfolio also tells me about the abilities of its designer to communicate ideas and
images in graphic form. Much like in a building, there is a great deal of freedom within

the physical limits set by the medium and the cultural limits set by convention, and I can tell about the judgment of the designers by how constrained they have been by these limits or by how much freedom they have taken with them. I can even judge how well they have managed their time in either overdoing the portfolio design or in having established an efficient process for preparing it.

Finally, I can see how all of these decisions have come together in a single object; that is, how coherent with the work illustrated is the form in which it is presented, and, just as important, how coherent is the portfolio with regard to the person that it represents. In the design of a portfolio I encounter many of the same issues, problems, skills, and talents that are necessary to produce architecture.

Cesar Pelli

ACKNOWLEDGMENTS

The third edition of this book could not have happened without the support of many people. I am deeply grateful to Robert A. M. Stern for his inspired front note and to Cesar Pelli for his insightful foreword, both of which reflect great humility, understanding, and keen perception of academic and professional experience. I am grateful to all of the design faculty, students, and professionals from across the United States, Canada, Puerto Rico, Europe, and Scandinavia who gave advice freely and were equally generous in lending work for previous—and this current—edition. Special thanks are due to Laura Clary, architect with HarleyEllis in Southfield, Michigan, for her generous advice and contributions. The chapters on digital strategies and digital directions are largely based on information she provided.

I am equally indebted to Steven Rost, associate professor of architecture at Lawrence Technological University, who took the photographs for the original book and this current edition, and provided material for the section on photography for portfolios (see chapter 2), as well as advice throughout. Also deserving of thanks are Paul Matelic and Julie Kim, principals of StudiozONE, llc., and Warehouse Productions, for their continuing support, generous advice on digital design, and for their portfolio contributions. I thank Margo Hutcheson, career coordinator at the College of Design, Iowa State University; Gail Liebhaber, of career services at the Graduate School of Design, Harvard University; Lee W. Waldrep, associate dean at the College of Architecture, University of Maryland; and Neville Clouten, retired dean of the College of Architecture and Design, Lawrence Technological University—all for their inspired commitment to design students' professional development.

I also thank Max Underwood, an architect and professor at Arizona State University; David Miller of Miller's Artist's Supply for outstanding graphic-production support; Matthew Coates, Ron Church, Dale Ihnken, Joshua Miller, and Nana Ekow Maison for suggestions and studio assistance; Maria Sieira, for her review and advice; and Robert Rowe, Associate Professor of Art, Bradley University, and Anthony Knaff for their design of my new Web site, www.portfoliodesign.com. Many thanks also to Jeffrey Huberman, dean, and James Ludwig, associate dean, both of the Slane College of Communications and Fine Arts at Bradley University, who inspire imagination and creativity in all that we do in our college—the Dream Factory. A very special thanks also to Jackie Bourscheidt, secretary to the dean's office, Joan H. Wilhelm, administrative assistant to the dean, and Mary Heintz, secretary of Slane College's Department of Art.

Thanks to my colleagues at the "Moral Science" table who inspire critical thinking, who zealously promote academic programs of professional development and international exposure, and who delight in the accomplishments of our graduates.

Thank you to Nancy Green, my editor at W. W. Norton & Company, for her unwavering belief in the value of this book for students and the profession, her patience and determination to see the book come to life, and for the enjoyment of working with a very talented editor.

Nothing would have been possible, however, without the love of my family, who helped to make the tough moments as delightful as they could be: Deeni, Josh, and Jonathan, and my parents, Ruth and Leonard, who instilled in me an appreciation for devotion to work.

PREFACE TO THE
THIRD EDITION

The third edition of *Portfolio Design* has been developed to include an expanded discussion of digital portfolios. The vast majority of design students and practitioners of architecture and environmental design disciplines are now creating portfolios electronically. While writing the third edition, I have corresponded with many university administrators, design professors, students, and professionals who agreed of the need for a greater discussion of the digital direction portfolio design is taking. I have introduced three new chapters—Portfolio Preparations, Digital Strategies: Images and Text, and Digital Directions—while retaining the basic information of portfolio development and layout design presented in the two previous editions.

I am also excited to introduce a new concept of professional review in which three complete student portfolios are presented and critiqued by three industry professionals: Tod Williams of Billie Tsien and Associates in New York, Peter Lynch of the Cranbrook Academy of Art in Bloomfield Hills, Michigan, and Francisco Gonzalez-Pulido of Murphy/Jahn Inc., Architects in Chicago. I thank the students, Robert Zirkle of Yale, Claire Imatani of The University of California, Berkeley, and Matt Vyverberg of the Georgia Institute of Technology, who bravely volunteered their work for objective review by three of the country's top architects. My thanks to the architects who supported both this new approach of portfolio review for the third edition, and the importance of portfolio creation in design education.

Creating a portfolio of your work for application to graduate school, employment, scholarships, fellowships, grants, internships, or employment is an exciting step in your professional career. A significant portion of my professional work has been devoted to helping architecture students and recent graduates organize their work into a unified and coherent portfolio with strong graphic sensibilities and an understated elegance. I have enjoyed giving lectures and workshops at Harvard, the University of Pennsylvania, the Illinois Institute of Technology, Illinois, Wisconsin, Iowa State, North Dakota,

Southern Illinois, Ball State, and Andrews Universities, the Michigan Design Center, the College of Creative Studies, Lawrence Technological University, the American Institute of Architecture Students Forum, and numerous other schools around the country and abroad. It has been my privilege to meet design students who are committed to architecture and allied design fields, and who have the desire to make a fine portfolio project.

In support of your professional goals and to help you deal successfully with the organization and design direction of your portfolio, I have created a new Web site, appropriately named www.portfoliodesign.com. Here you will find examples of portfolio designs taken from my lectures and workshops, as well as suggestions for layout strategies and resources for production. I have also included examples of professional marketing tools, such as print and electronic brochures, from architecture offices for further study. Finding good examples of graphic design can be as easy as visiting local design firms for sample brochures, or writing to offices whose designs you admire to request samples of their marketing instruments.

As you proceed to design a portfolio of your work, remember that this is an exciting time in your life to put yourself and your work forward. Your work is a reflection of everything that you have learned during your professional education in design. Give yourself enough time to brainstorm numerous designs and make mistakes along the way. Make several trial booklets of your work from photocopies to test how it can be best organized. Do not hesitate to revamp the overall layout and its contents until it flows easily and legibly. And don't forget to thoroughly enjoy the process of working on your portfolio every day.

INTRODUCTION

This book has been written for students and practitioners of architecture and the environmental design disciplines. Throughout the process of developing the project, I have had the pleasure of corresponding with many university administrators, design professors, and professionals who expressed their overwhelming support for a text about portfolio design for their students and graduates. This project has therefore benefited from the participation of universities from the United States, Canada, and Puerto Rico. More than thirty institutions submitted sample portfolios. I have also benefited from correspondence with the undergraduate, graduate, and postgraduate students whose work is represented here, and who have had recent experience assembling their portfolios for submission to graduate schools or in the pursuit of fellowship and employment opportunities. These students have recently had to undergo the portfolio review process, with all its attendant anxieties, and their work anticipates many of the problems that others will encounter as they learn the basics of portfolio construction and presentation. I have made an attempt to include as many sample pages from these "real world" examples as possible.

The portfolios in this book are, of course, a limited selection of the work being prepared by students of architecture, landscape design, interior design, urban design, and environmental design in nearly two hundred schools in North America. I can make no claim that this book is either complete or even truly representative. However, the student portfolios shown here are those that instructors and department heads believed to be distinctive and worthy of being shown in this collection, and I believe there are many lessons to be learned from them.

For two decades, I have been teaching and creating courses in portfolio design in architecture, art, and design schools both in the United States and abroad, adapting portfolio design to a range of education levels. I have designed the courses as a sophomore-year requirement, as an advanced studio elective for juniors and seniors, as a postgraduate course for students who have earned a master's degree, and as a two-day intensive workshop for mixed groups of art and design students. In every case, the course introduces the practices of portfolio design, including how to document one's work, and also offers students an opportunity to reflect on both layout and design as well as on their accomplishments. The sophomore-level course works as an introduction to the practices of portfolio design and provides an academic review of students' progress and readiness to proceed into upper-division coursework. The advanced studio course for juniors and seniors helps cap the students' previous experience and gives them an ideal opportunity to design and execute a full portfolio for graduate-school admissions, employment opportunities, and fellowship and grant proposals.

In teaching these courses I have become aware that many students entering their last years of study or graduating from a four-year degree program do not possess enough exposure to and experience in the portfolio design process. The subject of portfolio design in many architecture schools appears not to be thoroughly addressed. In general, very little graphic evidence has been assembled to demonstrate what portfolios are about, how they are created, and what alternative choices for design are available. In attempting to address this problem I have tried to bring together as many of the existing resources as possible. There are a number of publications devoted to portfolio design for commercial artists, graphic designers, and photographers, and they are listed in the Selected Bibliography. So far as I know, however, there has been no recent effort at summarizing the portfolio design process expressly for students of architecture and the allied disciplines.

During the months of research and contacting various institutions for portfolio samples to include in this book, I realized that many students have widely ranging creative approaches to portfolio preparation, including the design of the enclosing system and all of the samples within. The sample design portfolios gathered here reflect not only energy and commitment but also much talent and creativity. They offer many insights into today's creative practices of portfolio design, as well as an intriguing look at some innovative forms of enclosure and original strategies for layout and graphic presentation.

It is not my purpose to teach the techniques of cutting, pasting, and binding a portfolio, or the fine points of working with various art materials. Rather, my intention is to present an overview of the practices of portfolio design in architecture and environmental design; to present a variety of current portfolio examples to show the range of graphic possibilities now being explored for the organization and presentation of your work; and to discuss specific technical practices only as they relate to design concepts and the basic principles of portfolio presentation. I hope that the discussions and illustrations will provide you with insight into professional presentation practices that can help to make your work stand out and focus attention on the essential ideas behind that work. The examples have been selected for their clarity and impact. I have tried not to burden the text with technical details but to illustrate a multitude of graphic design alternatives and to show how the most varied strategies can work if informed by an original and creative impulse.

This book also brings together the shared experiences of many leading professionals and educators who have commented on the nature of portfolio practices, helping to make this project especially meaningful. Their willingness to explain the elements of planning, design, typography, binding, computer applications, reproduction processes, and philosophy of presentation is an act of faith that is deeply appreciated. The viewpoints of these designers and educators from across the country only serve to emphasize the importance of creating a strong portfolio.

The role of the portfolio in student and professional presentations has taken on new meaning with the advance of computer technology and digital reprographic systems. The combination of word processing and drawing programs gives even home PC users the equivalent of a complete desktop publishing system and the potential to produce well-designed camera-ready copy. Many architects and designers are now converting their work into digital formats by scanning images into electronic files and manipulating the output to suit their needs. Once in digital format, an image or a design may be altered in fresh and subtle ways, or it may be shown from many views in a simulated three-dimensional environment. A modern architecture portfolio may now include several high-density diskettes, or a CD-ROM, for a full video or multimedia presentation; it may even exist only electronically, on the Internet. For the moment, however, the traditional practices of demonstrating one's abilities in a print format remain strong. After all, draftsmanship and graphic design ability are essential skills for the architect preparing plans. But for the portfolio presentation, the more flexible and higher definition digital imagery of modern scanners and printers will soon challenge traditional print reproduction methods in terms of cost as well as creativity. This book explores some of the new computer techniques as they apply to portfolio design, and some examples are included.

During my two decades of teaching, I have encountered many different kinds of architecture, art, and design students. I have realized that the interests and experiences of young designers can vary widely. Some students do not discover their own talents and abilities until late in their education, while others discover their voice relatively quickly. Some students do not necessarily develop beyond a certain level of self-awareness, while others continue to make strides in all that they do. Design instructors are continually faced with the challenge of "getting through" to a diverse group of students with various levels of ability, commitment, and design experience. We want to give our students "real world exposure," as well as a positive desire to look beyond first impulses and experiment with different formats and possibilities. We also want to communicate the exhilaration associated with the search for one's own identity. Max Underwood, an architect, expresses keen insight into the nature of design education:

The professional training received in architectural schools and professional internships generally focuses upon the transfer of an established body of knowledge necessary for professional competency at a particular moment in time. Within three years after their professional training, many of the facts, skills, and tools that the student-architect learns are obsolete because of the rapid rate of change in contemporary practice. It is at this critical moment that young architects must rely on their education to shape their future professional growth and evolution. The education of individuals must empower them to realize their potential, allowing them to adapt, discover new ideas, and direct their own personal future.

Knowledgeable clients seek out the educated architect, rather than the trained architect, to propose answers to the unprecedented conditions of our rapidly changing world. Education must be more than professional training, it must educate the individual, and nurture a trajectory for the lifelong evolution and growth of an individual's talent, mind, and character.

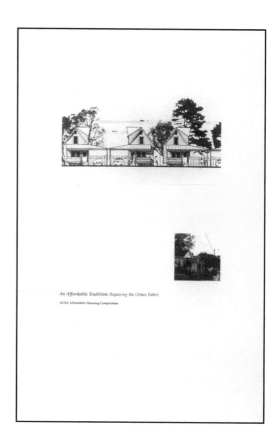

A simple, traditional portfolio layout using a
standard page size and a mixture of photographs,
sketches, elevations, and models mounted on
bristol card stock.
Dieatra Blackburn, North Carolina State
University, Raleigh, NC. 11" x 17"

An Affordable Tradition: Repairing the Urban Fabric

ACSA Affordable Housing Competition

This proposal addresses issues facing a decaying inner-city residential neighborhood in a mid-size town. In their present state of disrepair, the small, wood houses characteristic of this area exhibit a rich cultural and architectural heritage. The solution demonstrates respect for this history and contributes to their continued viability through a master plan which restores the density of the existing fabric through the introduction of affordable homes which interpret the existing architectural vocabulary. Both the master plan and the individual homes provide an architectural framework which enhances the physical and visual physical activity of the street vital in this area.

The project master plan and the form of the homes are derived from extensive site analysis and study of the local vernacular. Each house is sixteen feet wide and forty feet long with a corridor on one side linking the living spaces. The upper floor of the house is left unfinished and minimized to accommodate growing families. The front porch is an important extension of the house, a bridge between the individual and the community.

The proposal won first place in a national competition co-sponsored by the American Collegiate Schools of Architecture.

1.
What Is the
Design Portfolio?

Your portfolio is simply a collection of your best pieces of design work, arranged in such a way as to show your interests and talents as an architect or a designer, and the growth of those interests and talents over the course of your education and professional career. It showcases your accomplishments in the graphic form of text and illustrations, and it is usually enclosed in some kind of binder or case for protection and easy handling, or presented in a digital format such as a CD-ROM, DVD, or on a Web page. A finely tailored portfolio is the most important tool you can bring to an application for graduate school, a design grant, a competition, a job

The work in a design portfolio can act as a type of graphology or handwriting analysis, revealing the author's characteristics and personality, along with his or her design ability and character.

Bradford Grant
Chairperson
Professor of Architecture
Hampton University

interview, or to a potential client. In the course of your career, you will probably have to prepare many portfolios, each one adapted to one of these different purposes. In each case, your portfolio needs immediate and dramatic impact to distinguish you from others with whom you are competing, and it has to clearly answer the questions in the minds of those reviewing your work, for whatever purpose. The portfolio is a graphic history of your skills and accomplishments, and it must be seen not only as a work in design, but as a reflection of your understanding of the design process and as a tool to promote yourself to prospective employers and clients.

The challenge of proper self-promotion through portfolio design is to be able to objectively assess your strengths and accomplishments. Preparing a portfolio requires you to take a step back from your own design work and to make an evaluation as unemotionally as possible. Inviting the opinions of trusted advisors and colleagues also helps to eliminate the initial fears you may have about putting together a portfolio. Planning a portfolio presentation also requires a keen sense of organization and an ability to arrange various written and visual materials into a unified graphic package, as well as the ability to maintain a focused vision throughout the development of the presentation. Those who review your portfolio will be looking for a businesslike attitude and a pragmatic "soundness" in your work, as well as creativity and pure grace and beauty.

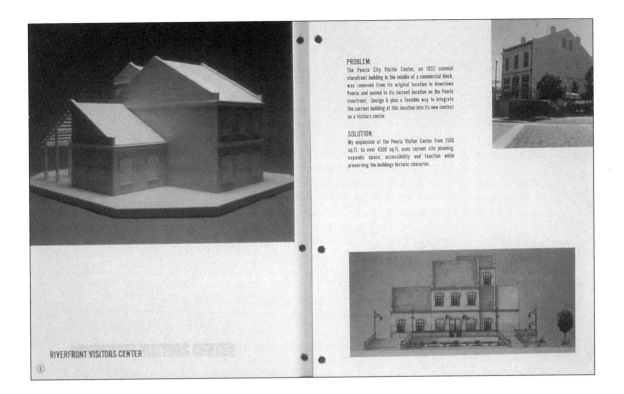

PROBLEM:
The Peoria City Visitor Center, an 1852 colonial storefront building in the middle of a commercial block, was removed from its original location in downtown Peoria and moved to its current location on the Peoria riverfront. Design & plan a feasible way to integrate the current building at this location into its new context as a visitors center.

SOLUTION:
My expansion of the Peoria Visitor Center from 1500 sq.ft. to over 4500 sq.ft. uses current site planning, expands space, accessibility and function while preserving the buildings historic character.

RIVERFRONT VISITORS CENTER

Plastics, aluminum, and plastic-coated paper form the enclosing system and contents for a bound portfolio entitled *Space, Function, Form.* Joshua Miller, Bradley University, Peoria, IL. 8" x 10"

Creativity is important, but a portfolio should also demonstrate a balance between a thoughtful design process and a promise to deliver the product.

Student designers with a creative future will have a natural curiosity about life and the world. Assembling a portfolio is an exercise that prepares you for future accomplishments in the real world by teaching you how to evaluate your own work, and to understand how that work will appear to other professionals. A good portfolio illustrates your strengths and demonstrates that you have a clear understanding of format, graphic design, typography, concept development, problem-solving, and business communication. Your portfolio not only represents a body of work acquired throughout academic and professional life, but it displays this work in such a way that your design philosophy is made manifest. Of course, most undergraduate

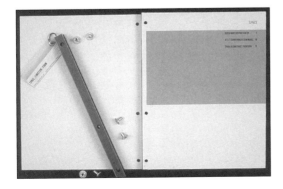

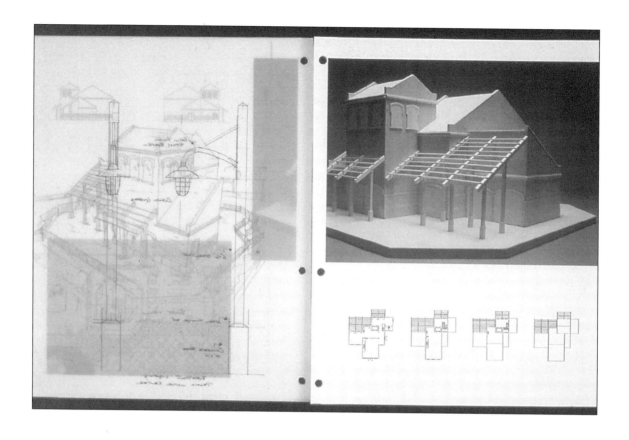

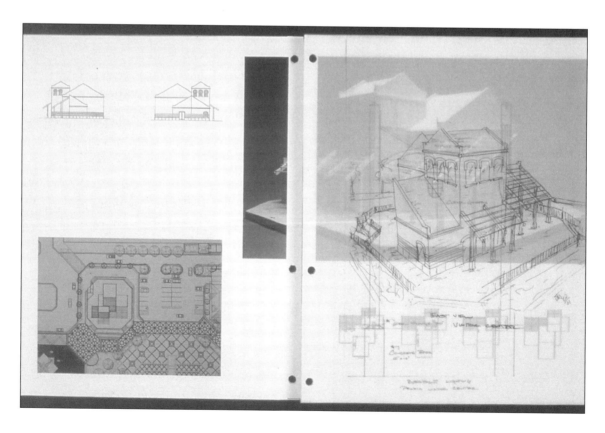

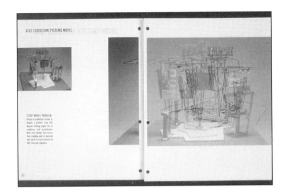

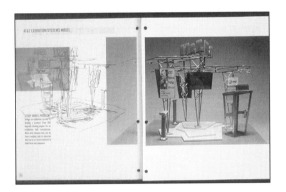

students have not chosen a specific area of design, nor perhaps developed a design philosophy, and tend to be generalists. This is not a drawback, because many good designers are generalists; they can solve any problem. Having a focus too early in your career can limit possibilities for growth and development. Your portfolio represents an evolution, not an end in itself. The educational experience involves growth, and growth often requires you to set aside prior knowledge to consider new concepts and directions. As Max Underwood says:

Great portfolios assist in our understanding of not only individual designers and their work, but their larger design vision and contributions in allowing us to see our world anew. One recalls the story of the arrival of Frank Lloyd Wright's Wasmuth portfolio in Peter Behrens' office, and work stopping for the rest of the day as the office staff of Le Corbusier, Mies Van der Rohe, Walter Gropius, et al. leafed through the pages and saw their modern world anew. . . . A quality portfolio is like a garden, constantly being watered for future nourishment and beauty.

There is no single formula for assembling a good portfolio. Not only will the thinking of architects and designers change in the course of their career, but portfolio objectives change. In applying for advanced study or a professional position, the goal may be to demonstrate a variety of interests, or a process of growth and learning over time. In applying for a specific grant or competition,

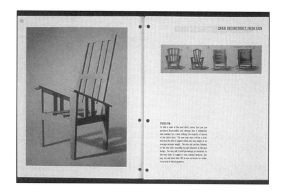

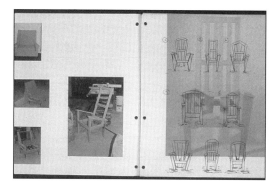

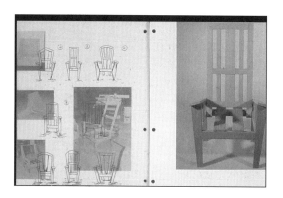

the goal may be to demonstrate knowledge and expertise in a specialized area known to be of interest to the grant or competition administrators. You need to identify your audience and guide your portfolio to reflect their objectives.

An effective portfolio presentation may be the only means of getting your foot in the door. Most professionals prefer to review an applicant's portfolio before scheduling a meeting. You drop off or send the portfolio to the reviewers before an interview, so it makes the all-important first impression. It must show everything that you want to show clearly and dramatically. It must be self-explanatory, and it must anticipate the concerns of the reviewers.

Following is a summary of the key considerations to which you will be introduced in this book. We will, first of all, talk about the need to establish habits of *documenting* your work from the beginning of your career, and the need to develop skills in photography to keep a record of your work. The selection of a photographic medium for documentation can include print, transparency, film, digital photography, scans from original work, and various other printing methods such as photocopying. The selection of a medium for presentation includes print portfolios, electronic portfolios, and hybrid forms.

We will then review the *objectives* of the portfolio. What is included in a portfolio largely depends, as I have said, on the audience it is intended for, and what you want to say to that audience about your work. What

A portfolio is, in many ways, a kind of window that opens up, not just the work of the student, but their manner of thinking. The way in which the material is presented, the evidence of a concern for the crafting of each element, suggest volumes about the character of the person who puts it together. An articulate, concise, and consciously crafted portfolio, even one which conveys unspectacular work, sets up concrete expectations about the student's thoroughness and attention to detail. These are the qualities most employers are seeking in an entry level architectural intern.

Roger Spears
Assistant Professor of Architecture
School of Design
North Carolina State University

skills do you want to emphasize, what areas do you enjoy working in, and how do you want to focus your interests in the future?

The objective guides the *portfolio audit*, the next step in the process. Here you select the projects for inclusion and do some basic editing, that is, decide how many pages of the portfolio should be devoted to each project, which pieces of work should represent the project and which should be excluded, what type of reproduction method would be appropriate for each piece, and what should be the order of the projects within the portfolio.

The next step is to decide upon the general *format* of the portfolio. The format is defined as the size and shape of the portfolio and its pages, and is determined by judgments made during the portfolio audit about the best way to present the projects you have chosen. The format may be vertical (or portrait), in which the pages have greater height than width, or horizontal (or landscape), in which the width is greater than the height, or square.

Once the size and construction of the pages is decided, we come to the question of the *enclosing system*. The enclosing system is the physical means by which the contents of the portfolio are stored and protected. It may be a commercial leather or vinyl folder with or without a loose-leaf or spiral binding mechanism, or a customized case made of cardboard, wood, metal, or another material. Of course, the enclosing system today could even be a small plastic box containing computer diskettes, or the diskettes might be

Cover and an interior spread of a portfolio with dramatic sepia-toned photographs. The format is a standard photographic size.
Andrew R. Tinucci, University of Illinois, Champaign-Urbana, IL. 8″ x 10″

included as part of a more conventional presentation. Whatever enclosing system you choose, the reviewer must be able to manipulate it easily and work his or her way through the presentation in a simple, straightforward manner.

From these basic decisions about form and size and content, we will move on to the complex subjects of *graphic design* and *page layout*. Graphic design refers to how we translate architectural concepts into easily understood terms on the printed page. Remember that the portfolio depends upon visual images to get its message across. In effect, its function is to tell a story without words, or with as few words as possible. You must now learn to think of structures not in terms of how they will stand on real sites, but how they will present themselves on the flat page, and how much of their ingenuity and complexity will be visible through different

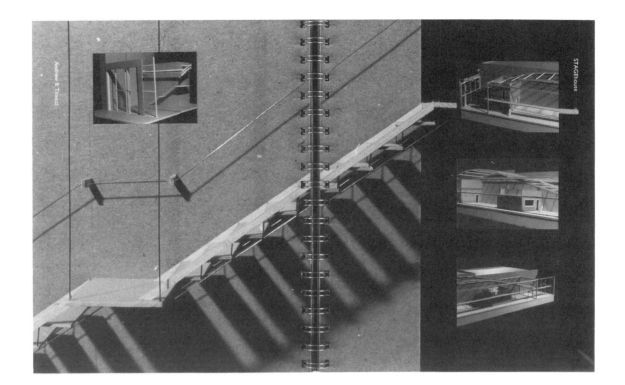

types of graphic—that is, printed (two-
dimensional)—media.

Page layout is a vast subject in its own
right, always evolving, and we can only
cover some basic principles in this book. We
will discuss the creation of a *grid*, an underlying structure or template that guides you
in positioning and scaling images and text
while helping to maintain a consistent design.

Page design is affected by decisions about
methods of reproduction made during the
portfolio audit. Depending upon the documentation available to you, you will have
decided how a particular piece of work
should be reproduced—through original art,
offset printing, photocopying, photography,
and scanning.

You must then consider text and captions,
for these elements bring out features of your
work that may not be obvious when a viewer

A comprehensive graphic-design study that includes cover, table of contents, design statement, and design projects. Note the careful analysis of content and image and positive and negative page space.
Keenie Fieger, Lawrence Technological University, Southfield, MI. 10″ x 10″

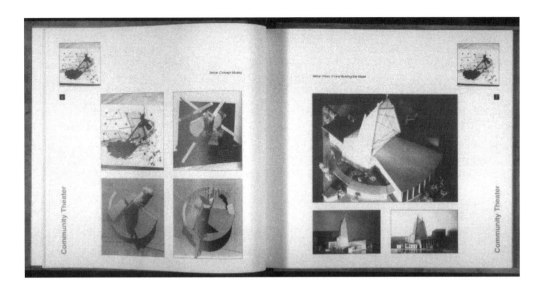

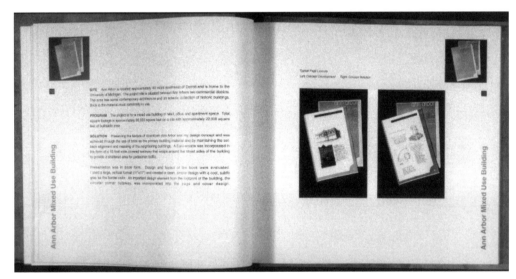

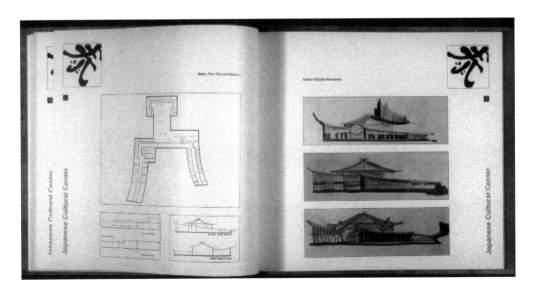

A boxed edition of plates large enough to
accommodate various types of documentation,
including photographs, printed text on transparent overlays, and double and triple-folded
panels.
Brita Brookes, University of Michigan,
Ann Arbor, MI. 9″ x 12″

looks at the graphic elements. To organize
the material selected, you may have a title
page, a table of contents, a page numbering
system (especially important with a series of
unbound plates), and even an index. The
goal, of course, is to make the portfolio easier
for the reviewer to comprehend.

After graphic design and page layout, we
will discuss the subtle matter of *sequencing.*
You have already decided upon the number
and general order of projects during the
portfolio audit, but what is the best way to
arrange the pages or plates within each

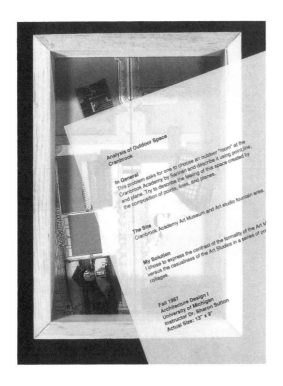

Analysis of Outdoor Space
Cranbrook

In General
This problem asks for one to choose an outdoor "room" at the
Cranbrook Academy by Sarinen and describe it using point,line,
and plane. Try to describe the feeling of this space created by
the composition of points, lines, and planes.

The Site
Cranbrook Academy Art Museum and Art studio fountain area.

My Solution
I chose to express the contrast of the formality of the Art Museum
versus the casualness of the Art Studios in a series of photo
collages.

Fall 1987
Architecture Design I
University of Michigan
Instructor Dr. Sharon Sutton
Actual Size: 13" x 9"

project, and how should you handle the transitions between projects? Sequencing is equivalent to editing in filmmaking, and concerns itself with how one thing follows another in a continuous or disconnected series of images, and how much space or "weight" is given to each element. A sequence may be governed by the changing size of the images or their growing complexity, evolving forms, or a change of scale or perspective. Sequencing is the process of deciding how many pages to devote to each project, how to build interest in the project, and how to make transitions between projects and yet maintain a consistent design.

To illustrate some of these basic concepts, let's take a look at several quite different approaches to portfolio design:

Joshua Miller, a design/sculpture student presented his undergraduate work in a bound portfolio designed from a kit of parts for mass production and easy assembly (pages 27–30). The portfolio emphasizes design process, with preliminary studies in graphic and three-dimensional form, finished models, and design methodology and development.

Architecture student Dieatra Blackburn prepared her portfolio in application for a traveling fellowship from Skidmore, Owings & Merrill. She focused on the problem of housing the homeless in hospices and private homes (pages 24–25). The portfolio consisted of unbound sheets of bristol board with photographs and text mounted directly on the board surface. Page numbers were clearly

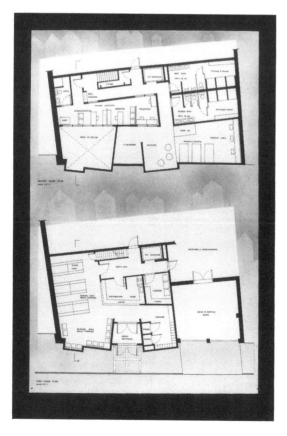

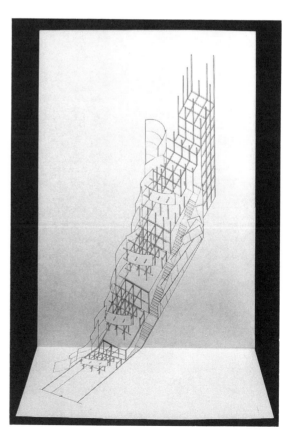

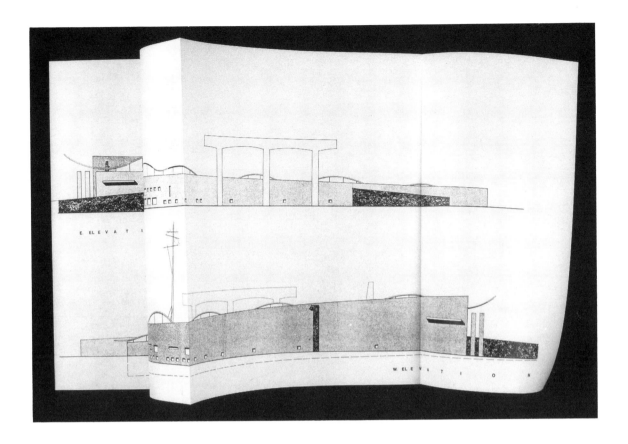

lettered on the reverse side of each plate, and the entire suite was placed into a ready-made box intended for archival photographs (not shown). Working with a page size of 11" x 17", set by SOM, Dieatra used an invisible grid to position the elements of each page in solid blocklike form. Negative space is used as effectively as printed space. This open area directs the eye toward the images, giving them importance beyond what their size would indicate. The use of negative space as a design element, with the images reduced and offset on the page, lends a quality of asymmetry and understatement that is very effective.

Andrew R. Tinucci's portfolio submission (pages 32–33) for a graduate program used a wire-bound format with sepia-toned prints adhered to the page surfaces. The double-

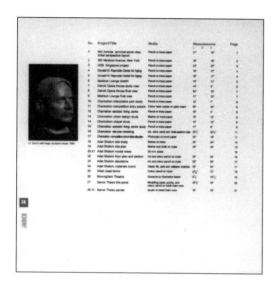

This index page shows a clearly arranged spreadsheet with corresponding portfolio page numbers and the titles, media, and size of each project.
Ron Church, Lawrence Technological University, Southfield, MI. 10" x 10"

page spread shows how he extended the design across the "gutter" (inner margins) of the portfolio. An interesting contrast is created through photomontage by using smaller photographs of details inset on the full-page images.

These portfolios reflect careful planning and forethought about how the portfolio will work as a whole. In the same way that animators and filmmakers storyboard their work before production, these students gave a great deal of attention to their overall designs to solve as many problems as possible before actually assembling their presentations.

The design process and the various steps described above are meant to help you pre-plan as many important elements as possible. The ability, so to speak, to see the finished sculpture inside the block of stone before the chisel is taken up saves enormous time and effort, and indicates both organization and creativity.

The illustrations on pages 34–35 are from the portfolio of Keenie Fieger, a former student in my senior portfolio course. Her pages were produced on a computer and illustrate a variety of typography, photography, drawing and drafting in a successful, open layout design. The cover is handmade. The computer desktop publishing system makes many styles of type available to the designer. In these samples, type is simple sans serif, which complements the visual materials in the portfolio. This layout includes the use of an invisible grid, which helps to position all of the materials, including small sketches and details, page

One of the most interesting aspects of our profession of architecture is that it is tangible. Drawings, models, and simulations are not only tools but artistic creations as well. A thoughtfully planned and skillfully executed portfolio is the best evidence of an individual's competence, skill, and talent. In evaluating future performance in academic or professional design activity, the portfolio remains the single most informative device.

Romolo Martemucci, AIA
Interim Department Head, Architecture
    Department
Pennsylvania State University

numbers, running heads, and project titles, and the important visual elements. The orchestration of these ingredients results in a rich dialogue between details and large images, process and product, in a unified and sophisticated presentation.

The portfolio of Brita Brookes (pages 36–39) illustrates the full range of creative techniques, design influences, and production processes that can be brought into play. She created three identical boxed sets of plates as part of a successful application to graduate school. The container is made of wood and the sliding lid is treated as a surface for collage portraiture. A wide variety of materials demonstrate the range of the designer's abilities, including assemblage and photo-collage, sketching, modeling, and drafting. All of the work is mounted on solid core black mat board as individual plates. Ms. Brookes created several three-dimensional constructions that were carefully illuminated, photographed, color-copied, and then mounted. Project statements were printed on translucent paper and included at selected points within the sequence of plates. Several pages with larger drawings were carefully sized to work as two-panel or three-panel foldouts. The size of the black mounting board is constant and permits changes in the size of the paper for individual presentations. This portfolio brings together different elements in a coordinated graphic package, and clearly reveals the designer's style, personal tastes, and professional interests.

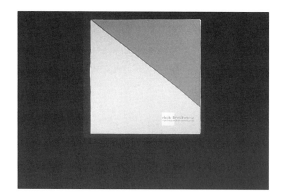

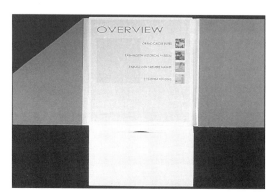

This plate portfolio with enclosed
CD-ROM was placed in a handcrafted box with folding panels and
graphic treatments including vellum
inserts to carry project titles and
statements.
Richard Lindbeck, Lawrence
Technological University, Southfield,
MI. 8″ x 8″

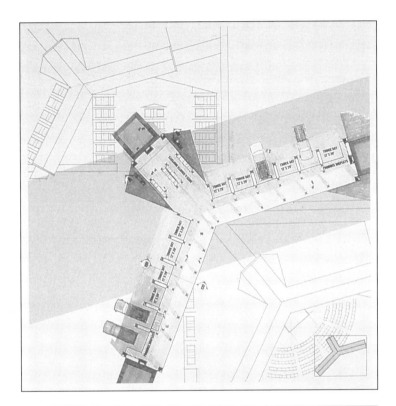

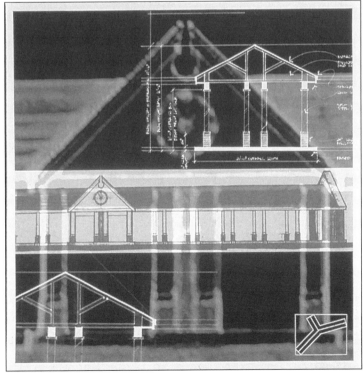

The portfolio is an important tool in every phase of our program. Students are required to prepare a portfolio of work completed in each studio from design fundamentals through thesis. Each studio instructor submits a portfolio of student work documenting each semester's results. Portfolios are required for admission into the five-year Bachelor of Architecture degree program. Portfolios form an essential component of virtually every decision I make.

Johnathan Friedman, Dean
School of Architecture
New York Institute of Technology

Sample pages from an undergraduate portfolio in architecture by Richard Lindbeck are shown on pages 42–43. The plate portfolio was designed in a handmade shallow box with graphic treatments on fold-out panels and a table of contents printed on vellum. The portfolio includes a CD-ROM with a PowerPoint demonstration of all of the work in the portfolio, as well as printed plates of his coursework in architectural design, design drawing, and computer modeling. Each section is introduced by a brief description printed on vellum inserts.

Francisco J. Gonzalez-Pulido's portfolio (pages 45–47) reflects the work of a talented student skilled in working with industrial materials and graphic design. The portfolio is made of stainless steel, with a lid like a music stand and two portfolio booklets, each of which can be placed on the lid's interior ledge for viewing. The graphic design was done on the computer with care to obtain transparent effects of printing, using translucent papers and subtle grays for type and graphic elements. The effect is a dazzling handwritten and handcrafted personal reflection on design accomplishment and the illuminated qualities of space in architecture.

Finally, let's look at the undergraduate portfolio of Matthew A. Flynn (pages 48–49), a student at the University of Illinois, Urbana-Champaign. The organization of this portfolio follows a successful pattern of placing architectural content in the beginning and following it with design projects and work-related experience to demonstrate artistic skill.

Freehand sketches and text created and edited in Lotus Word Pro are assembled on semi-transparent vellum pages and placed strategically between image spreads. The design of the portfolio is subtle and not cluttered with unnecessary elements.

A good portfolio also requires good writing skills as well as design ability, often the hardest element for visual people. You must demonstrate your ability to articulate in written form what your goals are. You must be able to write clear proposals and analyses of projects, as well as illustrate them. While the images carry the greatest weight, written communication is an essential business skill that must supplement your design abilities.

If you are enthusiastic about your work, you will find portfolio assembly an intriguing and creative activity. But it also involves hard

A handmade stainless steel container that opens like a music stand and two portfolio booklets make for a virtuoso performance; this is a highly visual and consummate graphic design and portfolio presentation.
Francisco J. Gonzalez-Pulido, Graduate School of Design, Harvard University, Cambridge, MA.
10″ x 13″

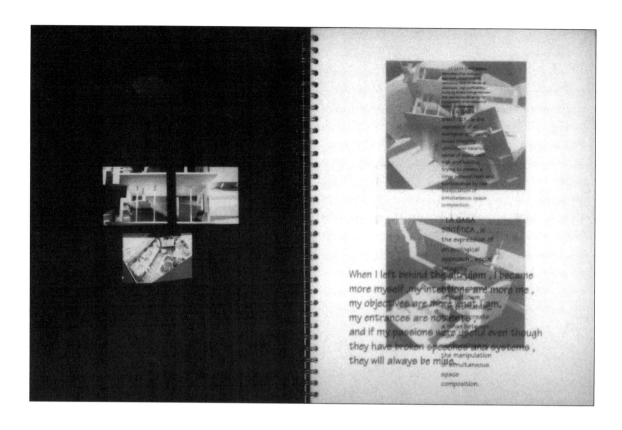

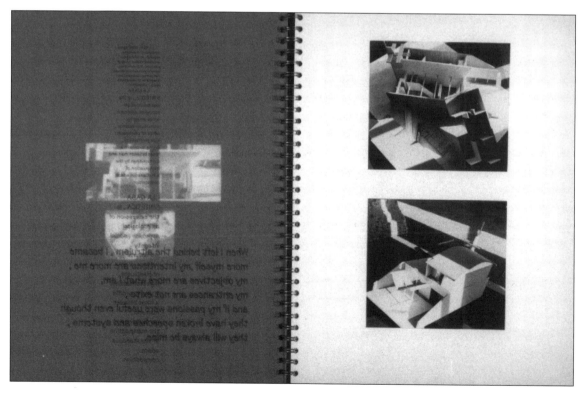

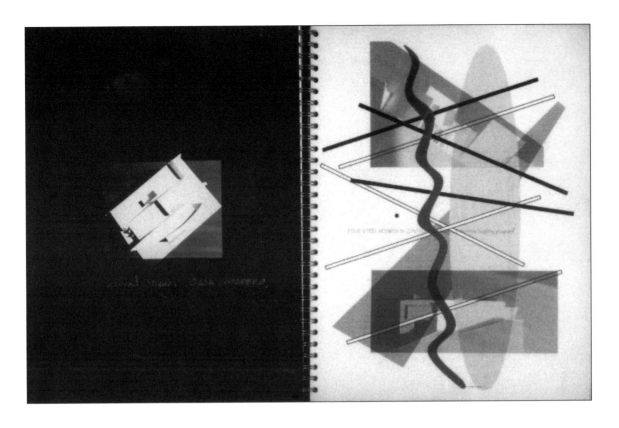

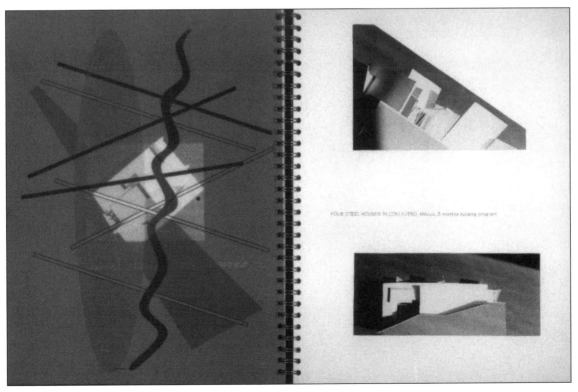

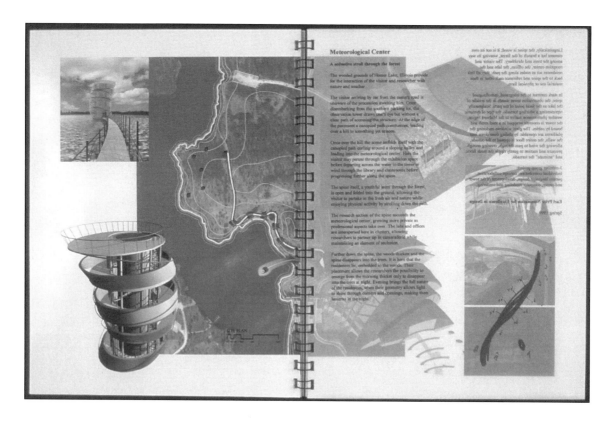

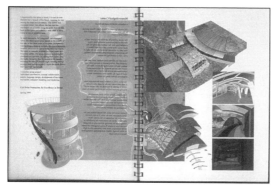

A diverse range of media and projects, including sketches, renderings, drafts, models, computer illustrations, and photographs is effectively organized into a crisp, clean presentation.
Matthew A. Flynn, University of Illinois, Urbana-Champaign, IL. 8 1/2″ x 11″

judgments. You must act like an editor as well as a creator. You must get your point across with a limited number of images, demonstrating your ability to be selective and critical. Every page or plate must build on the previous page by adding new ideas without redundancy, by expanding concepts, by taking a fresh approach to how the material is presented. You will then have a portfolio that sets you apart from the many others who are competing for the same job or academic program.

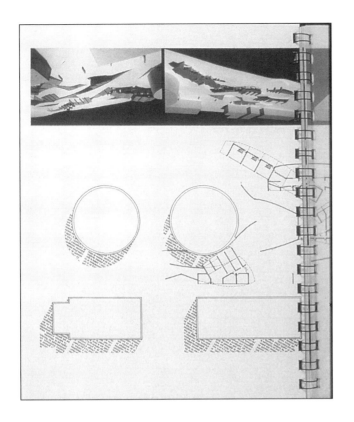

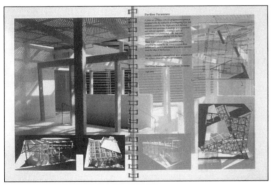

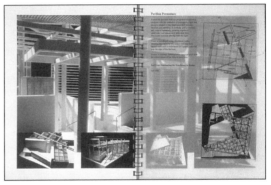

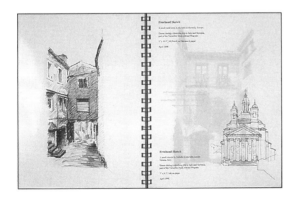

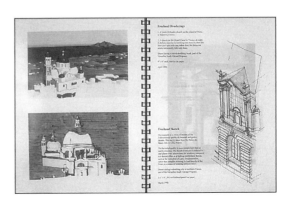

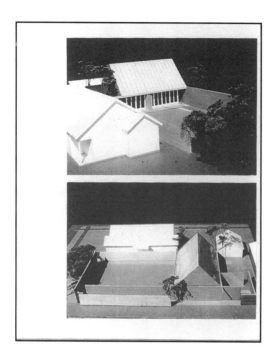

Professor Reese used indoor and outdoor
photography and graphics in these pages
from his professional portfolio.
Professor John Reese, University of Illinois,
Champaign-Urbana, IL. 8 1/2″ x 11″

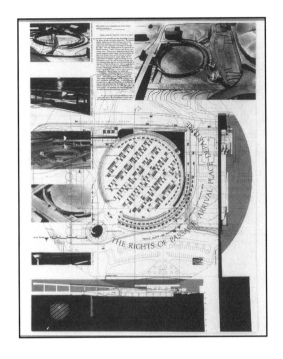

2.
Portfolio Preparations

Most two-dimensional design evidence in architecture and related design studio course-work is created on traditional supports such as illustration, mat and foam-core boards, mylar, and vellum at a size ranging from 18″ x 24″ to 20″ x 30″; the output from computer printers and plotters may be even larger. Because, for portability, portfolios are typically smaller in size than the original work, you need to select an appropriate method for reproduction, and usually, reduction. The four most common methods of reproduction for two-dimensional work are currently photography, printer output, photocopy, and photo-stat. The choice of method will depend partly on the nature of the original work and partly on economics (professional photography is expensive).

Photocopy original black and white two-dimensional work and text material; a range of colored papers, card stocks, transparent, translucent, and acetate sheets are available in standard sizes (8 1/2" x 11", 8 1/2" x 14", 11" x 17"). Large-format copy machines (over 11" x 17") are available in copy centers and companies that specialize in printing architectural and engineering drawings. You can photocopy on large sheets of mylar, vellum, and even illustration and mat board, or reduce the artwork in one or two steps to normal portfolio size.

Good photocopies and photostats are appropriate for work with a great deal of detail, such as construction documents, but be careful not to reduce the work so severely that the notes and dimensions become illegible. Original two-dimensional work created in black and white with high contrast can be photostatted or photocopied, in positive or negative. Original work with limited and very distinctive gray tones may also be photostatted or photocopied with a line screen.

Original two-dimensional work and all three-dimensional work (models) with values of gray (shading) must be photographed to retain tone—and in color, if color is to be reproduced. Many students use color copiers, and the quality has improved dramatically in recent years. Bubble-jet printers produce creditable reproductions, but color

Documentation of student work should begin very early in their academic career. Even though much of this work will eventually be edited and replaced, it is important to make those initial steps to record, photograph, and create the composition. Each successive update becomes more sophisticated. Drawings may be included if they clearly reflect the final design. The text should be clear, concise, and consistent in format.

Elizabeth J. Louden
Assistant Professor of Architecture
Texas Technological University

photographs remain sharper in image resolution and color fidelity.

As use of the computer in design spreads,
archiving of work done electronically, both
student and professional, is becoming more a
matter of course. But most students do not
work exclusively on the computer—and even
if they did, graphics consume a great deal of
memory. So for the present, remember continually to record your work in progress and
retain every sketch. Get in the habit early on
of reproducing all your work during the
process of creation and upon completion.
Models and constructions deteriorate over
time or are lost, and drawings and site plans
are difficult to preserve in pristine condition.
If possible, record your work while it is still
fresh, and keep more than one copy. Don't
discard your preliminary drawings: a selection of them belongs in your portfolio. Such
drawings convey your ability at problem-
solving, a skill that is more valuable to design
firms than a perfectly turned out portfolio
showing only finished work.

The need to record your work raises an
important consideration: how should you get
it photographed? Some students use the photographic services housed in their university
or college—these may be professional, a
work-study student setup, or a student-run
operation. Professional photographers offer
photographic and copy-stand services in
most cities; they are listed in the Yellow
Pages. Always ask for references, prices, and
samples before you retain the services of a
professional.

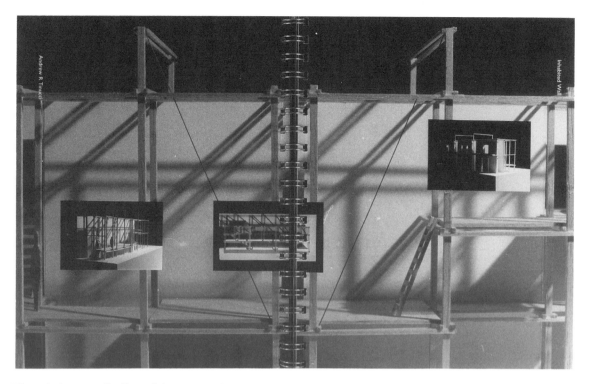

Though the overall effect of these pages is strongly photographic, architectural plans make a good foil for the dramatically lighted models. Andrew Tinucci, University of Illinois, Champaign-Urbana, IL. 8" x 10"

Even if you have your work photographed professionally, a working knowledge of photography and reprographic techniques is essential for any design student, and must be acquired fairly quickly after you begin professional study. Even if you are only ordering photographs, knowing how a 35mm camera or a larger format camera works, being familiar with digital photography, and understanding the photostat process will serve you well. If your photographs are made by a commercial studio, you must be familiar with the terminology of photography so you can give clear instructions to the photographer. Photographic literacy will eliminate misunderstandings and reduce your costs.

The best portfolio photography is done under studio conditions, with controlled lighting, with the camera held in a fixed position by a tripod, giving great flexibility in exposure times, depth of field, and perspective. Under such conditions, at least the photographer can be reasonably certain that the mistakes are his or her own.

The quality of photographic presentation in a portfolio is determined by several factors. It is essential, first of all, that the model, drawing, or item to be photographed be intelligently crafted and appropriate for inclusion. Photography flattens three-dimensional objects, and it takes some experimentation to see what happens to them when they are represented in two dimensions. While it is rare that a good photograph can make a poorly crafted work look good, a poor photograph can surely undermine the quality of a fine piece of work. The photograph must be sharp and reveal details, and must show the care that has been taken in designing the work. The biggest problem is controlling light and achieving proper illumination, best done in a photo studio. Large, flat pieces of artwork must be placed on a copy stand and photographed dead on, perfectly perpendicular, if they are not to be distorted and appear trapezoidal in shape. Models require a contrasting background because the materials they are made from rarely photograph with the strong contrasts of black and white art. Good photography requires you to make decisions about light and shadow, texture, depth of field (what is in or out of focus), and scale. Light can be manipulated so that shadows emphasize the geometry of the structure.Take details from photographs and enlarge them to make them clearer; lay the blow-ups over or next to the main image.

Visualizing a portfolio is in many ways a moment of introspection and self-criticism that any student has as a culmination of his or her architectural studies. Rational or emotional, portfolios have the particular sense of self-portraits.

German S. Martinez
Graduate Program Coordinator
School of Architecture
University of Puerto Rico

Though photographs or reproductions should be made as you are working on the projects, the decision about which views to include and how to position and crop them will be made in tandem with design and layout decisions during the process of preparing the portfolio, so that the whole page design makes sense.

The choice of photographic paper also offers many alternatives. A print can be made on warm- or cold-toned paper, on sepia-toned paper, or the print may be hand-colored with paints or pencils. Photographs can be mounted on white, black, or colored stock, with glossy, matte, pearl, or textured surfaces. Well-mounted photographs—whether adhered by dry mounting, spray adhesives, hot wax, or mucilage tabs—lend a presentation a custom-made, one-of-a-kind look.

Color photographs can give vibrancy to a portfolio, and are especially important for the presentation of interior architecture; see, for example, the portfolios shown on pages 65–68 and 101–104. Though transparencies produce sharper images than inexpensive color prints, they require special handling. As a rule of thumb, the larger the color film used, the better the reproduction. As a practical matter, however, the cameras necessary to use 8″ x 10″ film and the cost of processing it put these transparencies beyond the budget of the student designer. Even 4″ x 5″ transparencies may not be feasible. More common and accessible to students are 35mm slides. These are harder to view, since reviewers

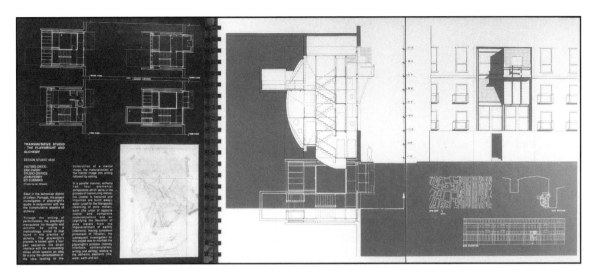

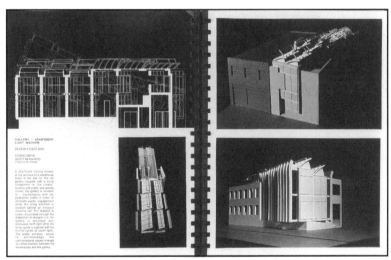

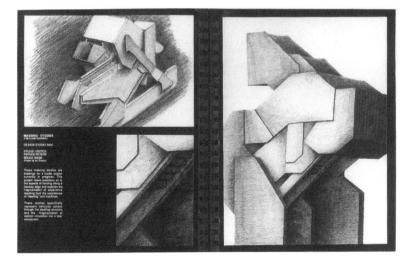

Positive and negative photostats and photographs make strong graphics.
Ian Scott Sheard, University of Houston, Houston, TX. 8 1/2" x 11"

may not have projection equipment available or want to take the time to set it up.

Transparencies are delicate and must be protected in some manner. Mount large ones under a black board with a cut-out window, with a sheet of clear protective acetate (mylar) over the slide. A sheet of translucent acetate placed behind the slide will diffuse any sharp lighting when the slide is held up for viewing.

Protect 35mm slides by inserting them in vinyl sleeves and be sure each slide is labeled and captioned. If you are taking them to an interview, don't expect the interviewer to provide projection equipment; bring along a loupe (a small magnifying lens that can be used to view slides against a light), a viewer, or a portable light box. Clean the dust from slides before you include them, and keep them clean (a can of compressed air and a soft brush, available from photographic supply stores, are useful for this purpose).

With the growing accessibility of computers and sophisticated software in the studio and at home, many more options are becoming available for the alteration of photographic images. However, the more you discover about how to manipulate images on the computer, the more you must keep in mind your final goal—to produce a high-quality, flat graphic image that works on the page. Follow the same principles of clarity and simplicity in designing computer images that you would follow without the computer. You may find that the computer is primarily

Your portfolio is not simply a representation of skill and experience nor is it a pictorial annotation to your resume. Your portfolio delivers a self-portrait of you as a designer: how you think, what your sensibilities are, what your process is, how cognizant you are of the design personality you are presenting and what you are trying to tell the viewer by the pieces you have included. The making of a portfolio is a design problem with a concept, a budget, a program, as well as a final product and a mechanism through which you communicate your individual design philosophy.

Patricia Belton Oliver, AIA, Chair
Department of Environmental Design
Art Center College of Design

valuable to you not in terms of original design, but to correct defects in photographic work. Poorly lighted areas can be digitally retouched, and color balance can be changed for greater contrast.

Composing page designs with more than one form of visual material—models, sketches, plans and other projections—can often assist the reviewer in understanding the project. For example, in Andrew Tinucci's portfolio (page 54) light has been manipulated so that the shadows emphasize the geometry of the models' structure. The professional portfolio of Professor John Reese (pages 50–51) shows, among other things, fine examples of how to present clear photographs and graphic reproductions. The design focuses attention on the illustrations by the use of a spacious layout and restrained typography. Ian Scott Sheard's portfolio (page 57) combines photographs and photostats with strong visual impact.

Assuming that you have a body of work to draw upon, the portfolio design process begins with an analysis of your objectives. Is this portfolio to be part of an application for advanced education, or employment, or for participation in an actual design project as part of a competition or a grant program? In general, a portfolio to be used as part of an application for admission to graduate school should show the broadest number of varied interests and aptitudes. For an employment application, this is probably an equally valid approach, though many architectural and

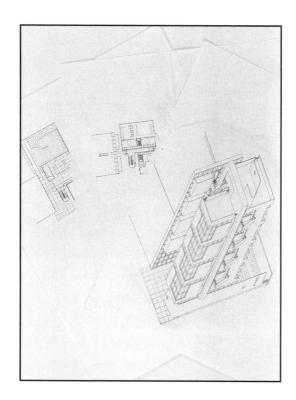

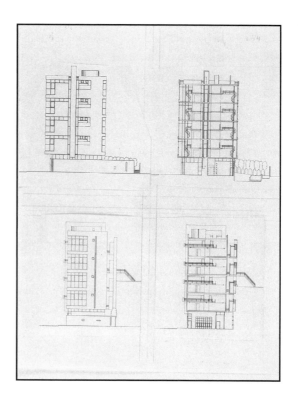

Varied materials, from conceptual
sketches and bubble diagrams to
finished renderings, perspectives,
models, and built structures, are
appropriate for inclusion in the
portfolio.
Alex Pugliese, New York Institute
of Technology, New York, NY.
8 1/2″ x 11″

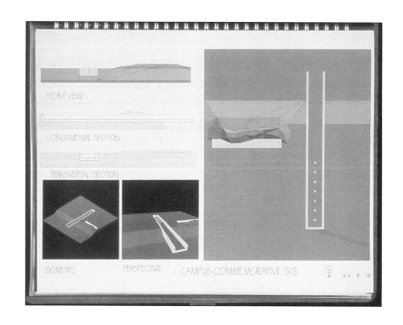

Numerous views of elevations
and perspectives are carefully
composed in this portfolio with
invisible grids in page layouts
using ArchiCAD and Photoshop.
Christie Ramos, Florida
International University, Coral
Gables, FL. 8 1/2″ x 11″

design firms specialize in a particular kind of work, and your knowledge of what the reviewers are looking for may help you to focus the selection of work more narrowly. Nevertheless, if you are looking for a job, a varied group of projects will convey the breadth of work that you can handle.

If you have been out of school for several years, it may not be wise to include school projects in a portfolio accompanying an application for employment unless the pieces are exceptional or especially relevant. Reviewers will want to see what you have been doing since you received your degree or became licensed. For a general portfolio, you should gradually replace school work with professional projects as they accumulate. It is appropriate to include a really fine undergraduate or graduate project, but make sure it is clear that you have been active since leaving school. (Bear in mind that the need to keep your portfolio up to date requires the choice of a flexible format and consistent methods of photographing or reproducing your work. If you begin with a small-sized looseleaf binding system and later find that a project intended for the portfolio is best represented on large-sized unbound sheets, you will be faced with assembling a whole new portfolio.)

In a portfolio designed to win a grant or competition, the focus will be narrow; you may be designing the entire portfolio around the solution to one architectural or design problem, or you may need to demonstrate your interest in and ideas about a single

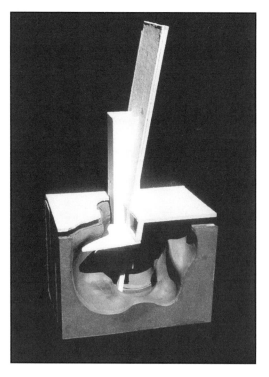

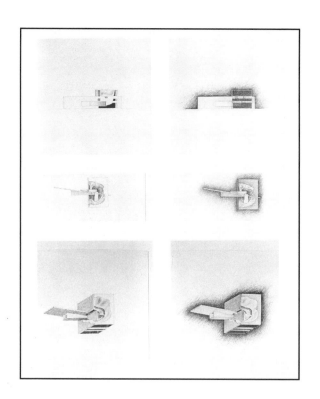

Piotr Redlinski, Pratt Institute, Brooklyn, NY.
8″ x 10″

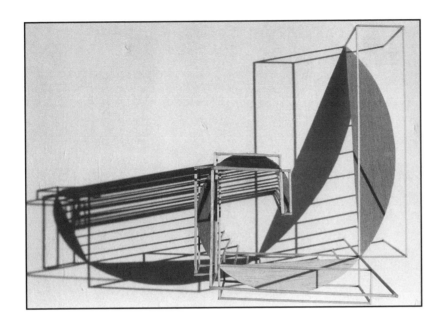

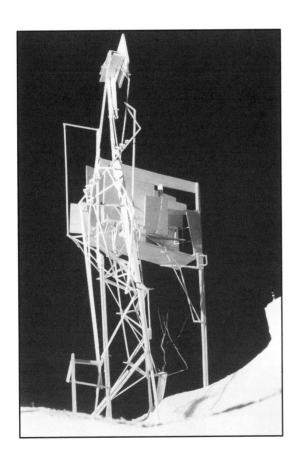

Design professionals, for the most part, rely on graphic images to communicate, record, and test ideas as well as solve problems. Through a wide range of visual media, I am able to quickly communicate and explore design images that are more expressive than words alone can convey. A well organized, representative body of work that reveals a diverse range of abilities demonstrates the depth of involvement of the designer. In this sense, a portfolio is an essential record of growth, as well as a vehicle of communication.

William Allen, Professor
Department of Architecture and Landscape
    Design
College of Architecture and Design
Lawrence Technological University

theme or issue. But even in this case, demonstrating a variety of design skills may be useful. Analyzing your portfolio objectives is important because you are preparing work to be judged by other people.

Once you have established your objectives, begin a portfolio audit. This is the process by which you select and, in preliminary fashion, arrange the work that you consider relevant to include. The form on page 70 (top) is one that my students use to get into the habit of making a thorough outline. Without preliminary notes of some kind, the coordination of all the details may seem an overwhelming task. On the "storyboard" form (page 70, bottom) students indicated in words and rough sketches an approximate sequence of projects and specific images.

The average portfolio contains at least twenty to forty pages (depending on whether you use single- or double-sided pages) that cover three to five separate projects—rarely fewer, but some portfolios may justifiably be more extensive. Too many samples reveal to reviewers an inability to be selective, as well as a lack of respect for their time; they may simply pass by an oversize portfolio without looking at it. In addition, carrying or shipping a portfolio that has become too heavy or bulky is a problem for you.

During the portfolio audit, lay out your work in piles on a table or floor, or place it in folders. Discard the weaker projects. Arrange what you have chosen in order of importance, and sort and select the pieces within each project.

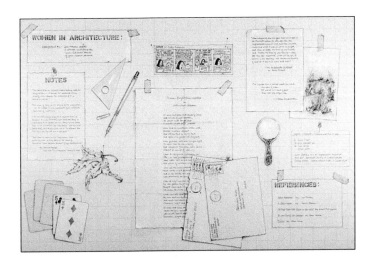

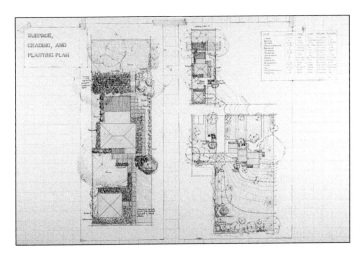

These design presentation boards present a collage of architectural elements in a soft and intriguing illusory space. These plates also exemplify graphic consistency of theme: the grid serves as a unifying element across the three plates.

Gretchen Rudy
Lawrence Technological University
Southfield, MI.

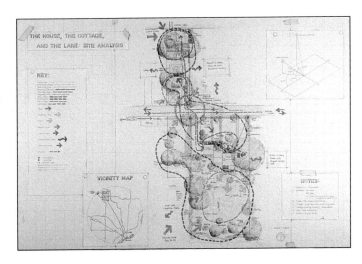

Interior and environmental design work for a senior thesis, "North Coast Harbor: Pier Park Development Concept," was presented in the form of a slide portfolio, a common practice among artists and designers. The selections shown here demonstrate the student's high-caliber rendering skills. From top to bottom, the retired steamship *USS William G. Matthew*, docked for dining at North Coast Harbor Pier Park; café *al fresco* aboard the transformed ship; and Pier Park overlooking Lake Erie; an aerial view of Pier Park, with North Coast Harbor and the Cleveland skyline visible in the distance; the seam of land and lake at Pier Park; and a model of Pier Park structures (1/8"=1'0").

Corbin Pulliam
Cleveland Institute of Art
Cleveland, OH.

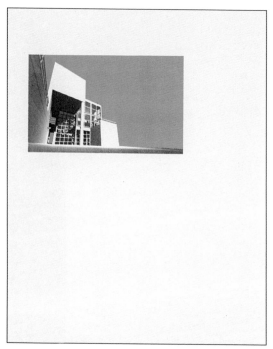

In this portfolio, a typographic first page of text is followed by a dramatic visual sequence in color. These computer-generated images begin with a small exterior view, positioned at the top of the page, and the images become successively larger or "closer" until an interior view dominates the page. The sequence demonstrates a remarkable sensitivity to the arts of animation and choreography.

Clive Lonstein, University of Miami, Miami, FL.

Think of the organization of your portfolio as building a bridge. Choose your very best work as the main supports. A strong piece of work should open the portfolio; another should support the middle of the presentation, and yet another should close the portfolio. The final impression is almost as important as the first impression; moreover, viewers often scan a portfolio from back to front, making the final piece of work the first that they see. The remaining work serves as the intermediate supports of your structure.

If you have enough work, an especially effective arrangement is to begin with two or three strong projects and end with one of equal weight, with the less important pieces in between. Sequencing is a complex issue we will take up in the next chapter, but during the audit you want to make certain that you devote the most space to your best work. If you have a strong project that was poorly executed (weak photography, sketching, or site plan, for example), redo it. Sometimes this is a difficult decision to make; as you grow more experienced, you will find that what once seemed like a strong project has lost its appeal, but that is part of the process of learning. And it is why your portfolio should be designed to be frequently updated and reassembled.

The advice to place strong projects in a particular location within a portfolio is not a license to put weak or poorly executed projects between them. Set aside weak projects. There should be nothing in the portfolio that

Two forms used in my portfolio classes to assist students in planning their portfolios. Preparing a thorough outline and storyboard of the work to be included is essential to avoid problems during the actual layout of the pages.

Generic shopping list of portfolio contents to be organized:
The following list should be altered , if necessary, to fit your specific content requirements.

Title Page

Opening Statement

Contents Page

Index

Art/Arch/Design Studio Coursework

Construction Documents

Computer-Aided Design & Drawing

Professional and/or Employment projects

Elective coursework

Your Work (School & Professional work)
In the space that follows, create a list of all items to be included in your portfolio. List these items in the specific sequence that they should appear in your portfolio. Once ordered, note your three strongest projects with an asterisk.

A portfolio audit form, with a reminder of the possible elements for a portfolio.

Portfolio Storyboard
Use the blocks below as pages of your portfolio. Label each page according to the sequenced list of contents you completed. Number the pages accordingly.

A portfolio storyboard.

you have to apologize for or explain, nothing that will cause the reviewer to wonder why it is there at all. You are choosing among your good projects and your best projects, and the harder that decision is to make, the more you can be sure you are on the right track. Nothing in your portfolio should be simply filler. Such inclusions are embarrassing and counterproductive. Professionals who review portfolios frequently say that one of the most common failings of graduates is to include too much work that is only average in quality.

Most portfolios are project oriented, but you can also add additional samples of particular kinds of work at the end if you want to show an area of special strength, such as sketches, watercolors, photography, models.

Overall, choose a variety of samples, from preliminary sketches to finished renderings to models, to represent each project (see, for example, the portfolios of Christie Ramos, pages 60-61, and Piotr Redlinski, pages 62-63). As noted earlier, reviewers appreciate the inclusion of conceptual drawings to show how your thinking has evolved. They are interested as much in concept development as the finished project.

As you audit your work, make preliminary notes about how to show each piece of work or each group of images. Whether on a simple list, a spreadsheet, or a storyboard, include the title of the project and list its component pieces, with planned sizes for the page or double-page spread. Note whether the items are drawings or photographs, and whether any special treatment, such as a

It is essential that students design their portfolios to impart a degree of individuality and personality. The student should not presuppose what an employer or institution wants to see; rather, the student should create a portfolio that defines what they, the student, want to say.

Tom DiSanto
Architect and Lecturer
College of Architecture and Environmental Design
California Polytechnic University

fold-out, is necessary. Note the appropriate reproduction method.

Include in the audit procedure what text materials are to be included: title page, table of contents, design statement, captions, index. A resume is appropriate if the portfolio is a general presentation of your work for further schooling or employment. A listing of course work, your employment history, and list of projects completed are possible inclusions.

Once you have selected a body of work, you can estimate the overall size of the portfolio, the number of pages or plates necessary, as well as consider what format and materials will work best and what type of enclosing system or binder is appropriate.

Many students explore a wide range of paper products in their search for innovative materials. Textured papers may be appropriate for original art. For mounting art, some use soft-colored papers in neutral gray and soft earth tones, and this may be a good approach for your work, but keep in mind that mounting graphics and text on colored or tinted paper can actually distract from the images and make the text harder to read. The most frequent choice is still white paper or board. Specialty materials such as translucent bond, translucent printing paper, translucent bristol, and transparent card stock are increasingly popular, because they offer a way to separate text from background visuals.

When you have made your choices about these issues, you can make a reasonable estimate of the art materials you will need—mat

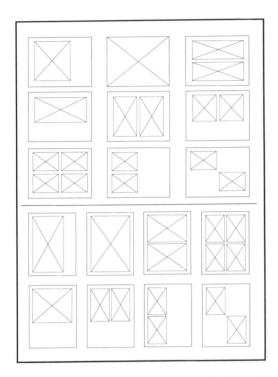

Sample thumbnail sketches, one for a horizontal format, the other for a vertical format, showing some possible layouts.

boards, acetate sheets, transfer type—and their cost. Plan to make at least one duplicate portfolio for yourself; more copies if you are making multiple submissions. Extra prints of photographs and a supply of extra art materials are useful to have on hand, since the portfolio may suffer some damage as it makes the rounds. (This may not be necessary for practice or "rehearsal" portfolios you prepare while learning to design them, but it is essential planning for the real world.)

Thumbnail layout sheets (see illustration) give you the opportunity to sketch out the relative size and position of the work you have selected in more detail than the storyboard. Careful thumbnailing prevents mistakes that could force you to abandon work at midpoint and start over from scratch.

Decisions about sizing art or photographs and the treatment of them depend upon the amount of detail they contain and their dramatic impact on the page. Reverse images—that is, white on black background—can be very effective for architectural plans, but at large sizes negative images can be overwhelming, and white type reproduced against a black background can be difficult to read. Photostats provide high contrast between black and white areas but reproduce areas of gray tone or shading poorly or not at all. You must match the reproduction technique to the artwork and decide what will work best for each image.

The portfolio audit is complete when you have assembled all the work to be included in the portfolio and have developed an idea of the order of projects within the presentation and the relative "weight" or emphasis that each project should receive. The more exact this is, the better, though it is common for problems and surprises to arise during the final assembly. Keep your audit notes at hand during all stages of the procedure. Like any other complex project, the more complete the plan, the easier the execution. The more thought you put into the audit process, the more likely it is that the portfolio will proceed quickly and without problems.

The next step is to fit the selected projects into a general format and choose the page size and enclosing system. The first decision is between vertical and horizontal formats; a less common alternative is a square format. Review your material and consider which orientation will give you the greatest freedom of design. Some materials demand a large, sweeping horizontal format to capture their scope; others require a large format of either orientation to permit the discovery of fine detail. Smaller formats offer handling convenience and perhaps greater intimacy, but require tighter organization. Students often use two facing vertical pages of medium size to create a large horizontal format, say 40" by 60," by planning the design to run across the gutter. What is gained here is the convenience of carrying and storing the portfolio in the smaller format, and expanding it for presentation. Never choose a format based on the idea that you can lay out some pages vertically and others horizontally, so that the viewer is forced to constantly twirl the port-folio around to read it.

The actual page size is determined in part by your design decisions and in part by your technical and financial resources. Will your pages or plates and your enclosing system be unusual and handcrafted, will you trim pages yourself to a nonstandard size; or will you depend upon standard, commercially available materials? Standard page sizes, available through most paper wholesalers, print shops, and photocopy centers, are 8 1/2" x 11", 11" x 14", and 11" x 17". Looking at your work, consider whether one of these will allow the viewer to see the de-tails as well as the full image. Review your portfolio audit and note the largest sizes of the visual materials that you have planned to include. This will generally point you toward the correct page size, though if one or two images must be sized significantly larger than the others, you might consider folding them down in a "gatefold" to fit in a portfolio designed for the average image size. It is simply a matter of determining the size of the largest element you wish to place in a con-tainer. If the largest piece fits, all the others will fit. Generally speaking, larger page sizes permit greater flexibility in placing individual elements and in creating effective photo-collages, groups of smaller images laid over larger ones.

The color, weight, and texture of the back-ground is important as well. A neutral color—white, black, and gray tones—usually works best. Earth tones and pastels can be used if

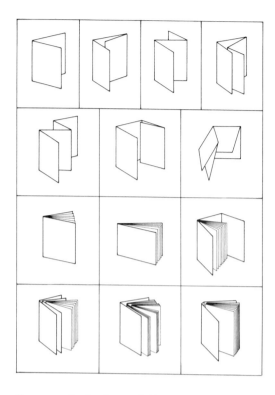

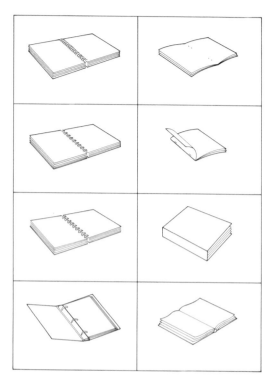

Seven methods of page folding: bifold, trifold (inward), trifold (zigzag), parallel, accordion, gatefold, cross fold; and six traditional bookbinding methods.

Eight traditional methods of binding: wire coil, sewn, double coil, side-stitched (stapled), comb, hinged folder, three-ring, adhesive (perfect) bound.

the circumstances are right; strong colors may detract from the impact of the images or create irritating contrasts. Whether you choose smooth or textured stock, paper or board, and other paper characteristics will depend on the content and format of your portfolio.

Format—the physical definition of your portfolio—includes the method of page construction and binding system. Most portfolios use one of the traditional book-binding systems (above); loose plates are less usual because of the packaging and sequencing problems they present.

Once you have determined the size of the pages or plates and format, it is time to choose an enclosing system. The enclosing system must be coordinated with the graphic design of the pages, as indeed it must also be related to format and binding. Although for purposes of discussion we deal with these items individually, all of them are interrelated and must be adjusted as the overall design develops.

The first question to ask yourself is whether the pages fit into commercially available binders. Commercially manufactured portfolio cases come in a number of standard sizes designed to conform to standard paper sizes. They are convenient, widely accepted among those who review portfolios, and certainly no more expensive than the art materials required to handcraft your own container. For this reason, most students and young professionals choose the common 8 1/2" x 11" page size, for which there are many binders available. One frequently used strategy is to prepare reproductions of highly detailed drawings, such as construction documents, in the larger 8 1/2" x 14" or 11" x 17" format and then double- or triple-fold them into the standard 8 1/2" x 11" acetate inserts that fit the commercial binders. Most commercially manufactured cases are sold with these acetate sheets, and you can purchase them from several manufacturers. You can cut open these acetate inserts to customize the insertion of 8 1/2" x 14" or 11" x 17" vertical or horizontal formats.

Though you may not want to include original drawings if your portfolio is going to circulate out of your hands, reviewers like to see original art. If you use originals, you should protect them by placing them in acetate sleeves, or between die-cut boards, or simply by slipping a piece of translucent paper between the sheets of drawing paper. Sleeves add a reflective barrier that makes viewing of the artwork more difficult, and acetate tears easily. Stronger plastic protective sleeves are available, but translucent rather than transparent ones, fine for holding slides, are unsuitable since they obscure the art.

Most portfolios are either 8 1/2" x 11" or the size of another commercial binder, or custom-bound in a box or a handmade binder. A large or nonstandard page size will almost certainly compel you to use a binder, box, or container that you construct yourself, but there are other good reasons to choose unconventional page sizes and noncommercial binders. You can size images with much greater freedom, and the work will look less confined. Nonstandard or oversize pages stand out. However, if your portfolio is oversize, be sure that the pages are securely attached or that the binding is adequate to support them. Pages that fall to the floor are soon damaged. And in choosing an unusual format, be reasonable. If you can't comfortably carry and view your portfolio, neither will anyone else.

A number of nonstandard and handcrafted enclosing systems are shown on pages 79, 80, and 81. Several loose-leaf-style binders are shown, as well as some elegant methods of enclosing unbound plates. Brad Burkhardt, an environmental design student,

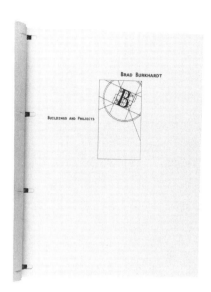

A handmade aluminum binder.
Brad Burkhardt, Parsons School of Design,
New York, NY. 10″ x 14″

put his portfolio in a handmade aluminum case. Jason Foster used an 8 1/2″ x 11″ card stock cut to 2 3/4″ x 5 1/2″ to form a mini-portfolio of a series of cards contained in a custom-made vellum envelope. Projects and text were carefully chosen for legibility at the reduced size format. Joshua Beck adhered to the strict submission requirement for portfolios at the University of California, Berkeley: twelve single- or double-sided pages, no larger than 8 1/2″ x 11″ (name on the front or back of each sheet), attached in one corner with a single staple. His successful presentation of well-composed sheets brought him the Malcolm Reynolds Prize for new Master of Architecture students.

In choosing an enclosing system, look for simple, stable, and sturdy construction. A binder that falls apart in the hands of the reviewer or is difficult to handle makes a poor impression. Your portfolio will be passed

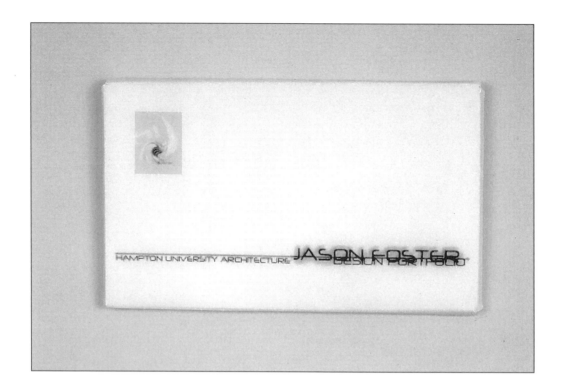

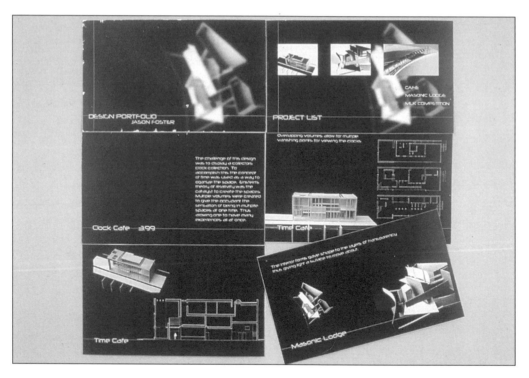

A mini-portfolio consists of small plates made from semi-gloss card stock and a 50 lb. vellum cover stock.

Jason Foster, Hampton University, Hampton, VA. 8 1/2" x 11" (cut to size)

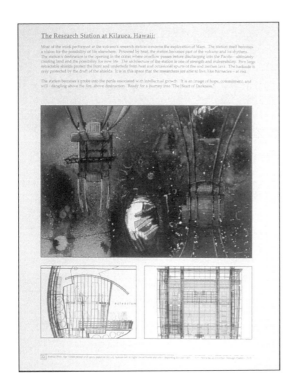

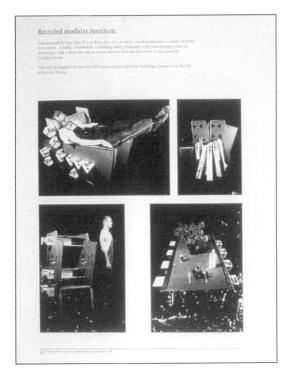

A series of carefully composed sheets contains all of the necessary design elements
for application to graduate school.
Joshua Beck, University of California-Berkeley, Berkeley, CA. 8 1/2" x 11"

around to many people and may not always be treated gently. It must be designed to endure use, and you must maintain it. A defective mechanism in the binder will irritate those who must open it, and denotes a lack of professionalism. Spiral or permanent binders are more suitable for a "dedicated" project that is unlikely to need updating. With bound pages, both sides of the paper are generally used. Unbound plates or ring binders make it easy to rearrange or add new projects over the years. With unbound plates, you will probably reproduce images only on one side of the page, and this may be costly in terms of available space. Unbound plates may also get out of order: if you choose this style, be sure that they are clearly numbered.

In terms of style, the enclosing system should be visually appealing but understated in a simple and tasteful way. It should reveal both a sense of imagination and serious professionalism. The materials, the color, the finish, the detailing should be striking, but not garish. The package should not be more exciting than its contents. Most commercial binders are businesslike in design. Hand-made enclosing systems provide the greatest opportunity for creative experiment, and the greatest opportunity for error. Pay particular attention to the sturdiness of the design and the materials if you are crafting your own case.

The enclosing system you choose also has a bearing on the sequencing of material. The double-page spreads of a binder force you to consider exactly how long each section of the

Limited resources should not be a deterrent to putting forth the maximum effort when designing a portfolio. The use of basic materials in a well-designed product indicates many things—among them creativity and thoughtfulness.

Kathryn T. Prigmore, AIA
Associate Dean
School of Architecture and Planning
Howard University

portfolio will be and how each piece of work will lay out. If one project ends on a verso (left-hand) page, what is the effect on the spread of starting a dramatically different project on the recto (right-hand) page? The number of pages devoted to each section may have to be modified to take facing-page design into account. Clearly, unbound pages avoid this problem and offer you more flexibility in arranging work, but with this arrangement you lose the option of expanding or enlarging particular elements to run across two pages. It should be obvious that you cannot prepare a portfolio in a completely linear fashion, dealing with only one design element or one decision at a time. You must learn to think not only in terms of what to include, but also in terms of how everything will fit and how consecutive pieces of work will flow into each other.

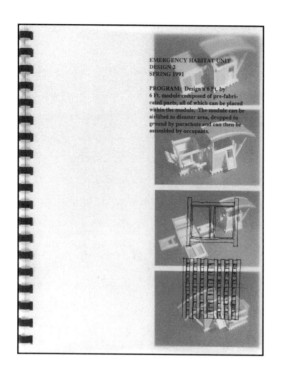

EMERGENCY HABITAT UNIT
DESIGN 2
SPRING 1991

PROGRAM: Design a 6 Ft. by
6 Ft. module composed of pre-fabri-
cated parts, all of which can be placed
within the module. The module can be
airlifted to disaster area, dropped to
ground by parachute and can then be
assembled by occupants.

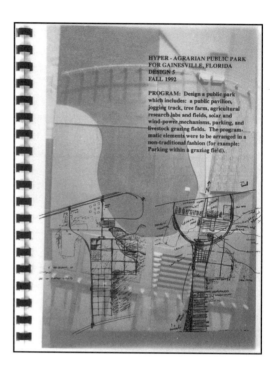

HYPER - AGRARIAN PUBLIC PARK
FOR GAINESVILLE, FLORIDA
DESIGN 5
FALL 1992

PROGRAM: Design a public park
which includes: a public pavilion,
jogging track, tree farm, agricultural
research labs and fields, solar and
wind-power mechanisms, parking, and
livestock grazing fields. The program-
matic elements were to be arranged in a
non-traditional fashion (for example:
Parking within a grazing field).

Translucent pages offer the opportunity to overlay
conceptual sketches and text on developed models.
J. W. Tisdale, University of Florida, Gainesville, FL.
8 1/2″ x 11″

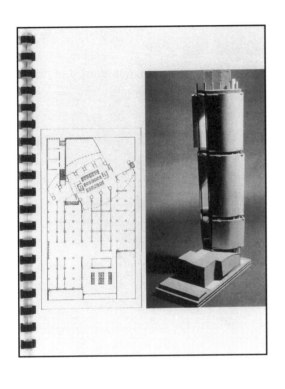

3.
Developing
the Layout

Let's first begin by discussing a few early decisions and suggestions that will help you develop your layout design carefully and efficiently. Thumbnail layout sheets like those on pages 73, 86, and 87 give you the opportunity to sketch out the relative size and position of the work you have selected in more detail than the storyboard. Careful thumbnailing will prevent mistakes that could force you to abandon work at midpoint and start over from scratch.

Once you have decided on portfolio content, general format, page size, and enclosing system, you now come to the vital matter of developing the layout—that is, designing the pages, sizing the images and placing them on the pages,

Eight ways of aranging columns of text
on horizontal and vertical formats.

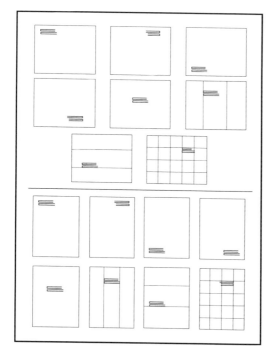

Eight ways of arranging heads
on horizontal and vertical formats.

designing the typography for the accompanying text, and creating the text elements such
as the title page, contents, design statements,
and resume, and fine-tuning the sequencing
or arrangement of pages within and between
projects.

Begin by designing a grid, or underlying
structure. The grid helps you to size and position the images in a coherent design. It is
really a set of assumptions about the permis-
sible sizes and shapes of images and blocks
of text and it helps you achieve some design
consistency throughout the portfolio. It is cus-
tomary to decide upon a standard "measure"
or width for the material. Text and images
may run across the entire width of the page,
or the page may be divided into two, three,
or more columns. The grid should take into
consideration the character of the images:
some demand large-scale reproduction; others can be reproduced small. For example,
you may want to group images in sequence,
showing the evolution of a concept. Break
down the pages into imaginary blocks of space
of stylistically-related appearance, and fit images and text into these blocks. Now you can
determine the final size and position of the
artwork. Using the thumbnail layouts you prepared during formatting, analyze the different
images and text blocks for each project and
each page and position them on the grid. You
may need to make a series of sketches, first
perhaps in the form of roughs on smaller-size
sheets, working up to a full-size "dummy" on
tracing paper. This is a process of trial and error
and constant adjustment to solve conceptual

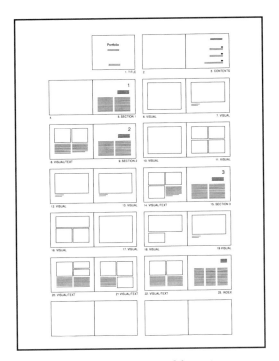

Sample layouts for a horizontal format
with headings, text, and visuals.

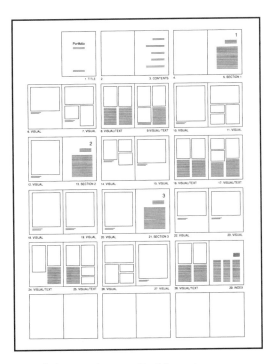

Sample layouts for a vertical format
with headings, text, and visuals.

problems that reveal themselves as you lay out the pages. Remember that the grid of a well-organized page should be essentially invisible: it should be a guide, not a strait-jacket.

It is during this development that the difficult-to-define qualities of style and vision evolve. For an important portfolio, you may want to experiment with as many as six different rehearsal studies of this kind. Working with full-scale tracing paper allows you to test the proposed size of each image against the page and see the effects of juxtaposition and sequence.

You can resize images easily with a proportional scale (available at most art-supply stores). The scale tells you, if images are being enlarged or reduced to a certain height, just what the width of that image will be in the new size, or if a particular width is desired, just what the new height of the image will be. Even easier, draw a diagonal line from one corner of the image to the opposite corner (on an overlay or photocopy: don't draw on original art or a photograph!), or extend the diagonal line beyond the border of the image. Any point on this line will produce a different-sized image that remains proportional to the original image (see overleaf).

As you develop the page layout from sketch to actuality, you make more detailed decisions about the size and style of text type, heads, captions, tabular materials, charts, and folios (page or plate numbers). Seldom are all these elements necessary: choose what you need to make your points. Is a project based on a class

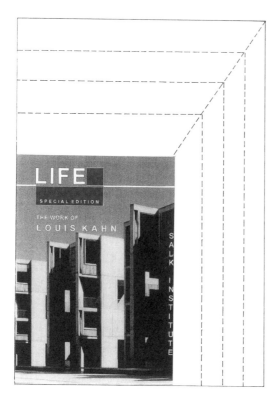

Simple method of enlarging or reducing artwork.

A portfolio is an opportunity to showcase what you have done and how you did it. It also gives the reviewer a real sense of what you are capable of doing. Simple or complex, it needs to reflect how you think and who you are.

Arthur L. Kaha, AIA
School of Architecture
University of Illinois at Urbana-Champaign

assignment or other coursework? Is a design statement helpful? Do captions repeat what is obvious in the illustrations, or offer additional information? Are relationships between visuals clear? Do details need explanation? If your portfolio consists of unbound plates, are they numbered? And don't forget that you must clearly label your portfolio, inside and out, with your name, address, and telephone number. It is counterproductive, to say the least, to submit a portfolio for review if the reviewers have no way of contacting you or returning your presentation!

There are many options for the placement of text elements. Legibility is a prime concern; text should work with the graphic images and not compete with or obscure them. Keep the text clearly separate from the images, or maintain strong contrast between their values in order to preserve legibility of both. Serif typefaces are elegant; sans-serif typefaces tend to be functional and businesslike. Highly styled typefaces may be appropriate for heads, but generally make for poor readability. While there are thousands of typefaces available, most of them suitable for heads under some circumstances, perhaps only a dozen families of type are really suitable for extended blocks of text. Study the typefaces used in books and magazine articles, and you will see the same faces again and again. A flamboyant or overly styled face irritates and tires the eye very quickly in long blocks. Does the type and headline style that works well for one project work equally well for all the projects? Is the design consistent? Refine the presentation.

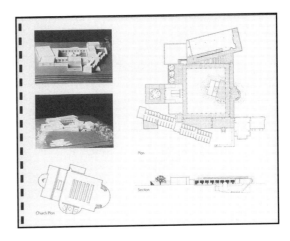

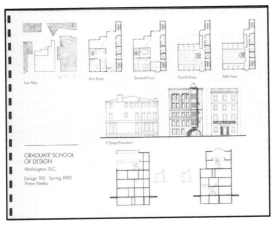

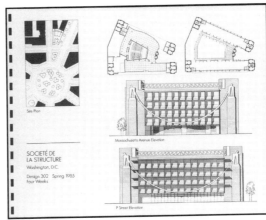

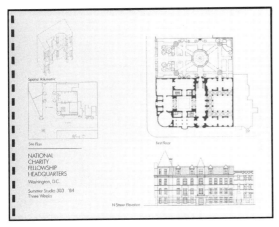

A simple but carefully constructed two-column layout.
Arthur Hanlon, The Catholic University of America, Washington, DC. 11″ x 8 1/2″

Five varied portfolios demonstrate consistent designs with different types of images fitted into a grid structure. Arthur Hanlon's has a horizontal format and a formal two-column vertical structure (this page). The vertical column on the left side of the page is narrower than the column on the right side of

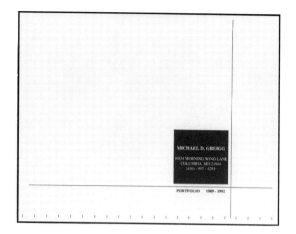

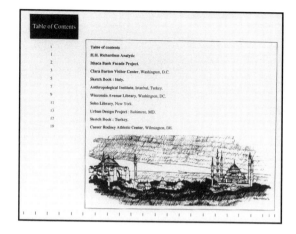

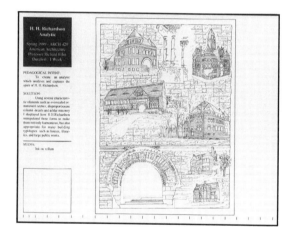

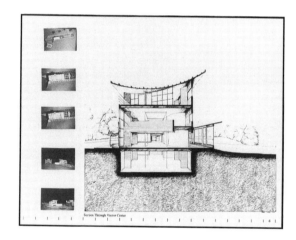

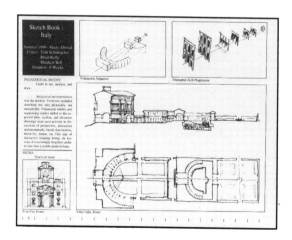

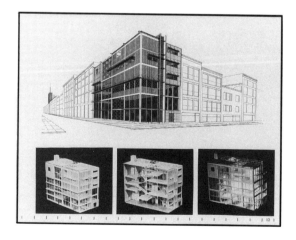

A flexible three-column grid.
Michael D. Greigg, University of Maryland, Columbia, MD. 11" x 8 1/2"

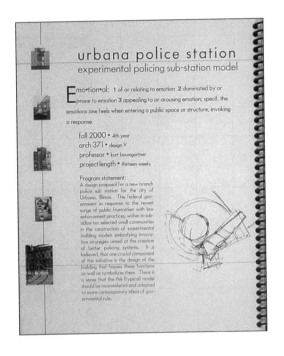

Highly legible layout design is based on the careful ratio of image to text and the alignment of both to a visible grid.
James C. Nelson, University of Illinois, Urbana-Champaign, IL. 8 1/2" x 11"

the page. But even with this highly structured approach, there is a sense of freedom in the design, created by the flexible way the images are laid out within the grid.

Michael D. Greigg's grid has three columns on a horizontal format (opposite). The page is divided into a fairly narrow left-hand column, used largely for text material, and two right-hand columns that can function as one wider column, as desired. In this way, he gained a great deal of flexibility with the right side of the page, which is used for large images or groups of smaller ones.

The portfolio of James C. Nelson (left) uses a grid structure to create visual intrigue and to align images and text. The combination of simple, effective typography and large images on an 8 1/2" x 11" vertical format results in a dynamic page composition and high legibility. Double-page spreads and gatefold pages that open to 11" x 17" are also included.

Carlos Brun began with a transparent overlay of typographic elements that also defines the grid pattern for the smaller peripheral graphic images on subsequent pages (page 92). Text and photographs are laid on top of other images at an angle to break the rigidity of the grid pattern and convey a feeling of openness and drama.

Eric Robert Jacoby used a three-column page structure and creatively arranged the images, text, and details throughout the sequence of pages in the layout design. The black background in the first column introduces contrast as a design element and raises

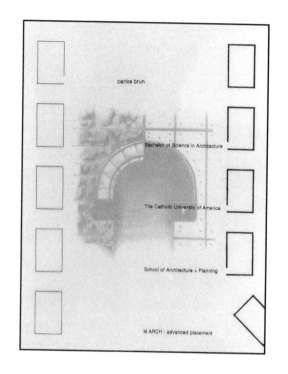

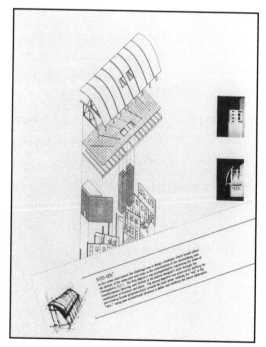

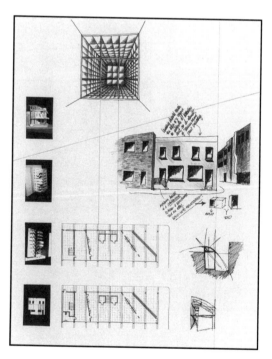

In this portfolio, submitted in application to a graduate program, the subtle grid is skillfully interrupted with diagonals to create a memorable sequence of lively graphic statements.
Carlos Brun, University of Miami, Coral Gables, FL. 8 1/2″ x 11″

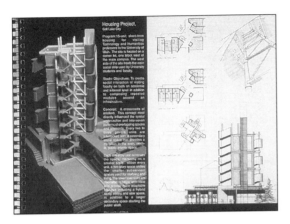

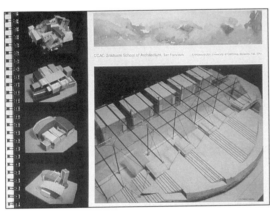

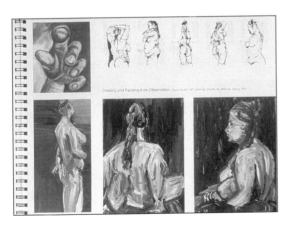

A portfolio design created in AutoCAD, Photoshop, and PageMaker on 11″ x 17″ sheets and trimmed to 8 1/2″ x 11″ to preserve a full-page bleed format.
Eric Robert Jacoby, University of Utah, Salt Lake City, UT. 8 1/2″ x 11″

the level of visual interest while increasing the presentation's legibility.

Four rehearsal portfolios (pages 94–97) illustrate still other solutions. Candace Law's portfolio of plates has an enclosing folder system to organize the evidence of her design process and project solutions for work in architectural illustration. The simplicity of her page layout and type design underscores the importance of visual evidence and artwork in her approach.

Adam C. Pew created a handmade box with chipboard, art paper, and corrugated paper laminated to the interior faces. He employed bifold and trifold plates for his design projects. A translucent page of explanatory notes accompanies each design project.

In his portfolio, Matthew Coates used a vertical format with text overlays and folded panels, with identifying text placed within a black panel on the left margin.

Karl Muegge made a series of individual booklets representing each of his design projects; these are inserted into a handmade cover box to complete the overall graphic package.

In Taha Al-Douri's imaginative and graphically sophisticated portfolio, the images are sensitively composed within the black foam-core rectangular mount (page 98). The use of the 35mm frame is a unifying feature.

The portfolio of James P. Ryan Associates, specialists in the design and construction of large shopping malls, was printed in four colors using special inks with a metallic finish, superimposed photographic images,

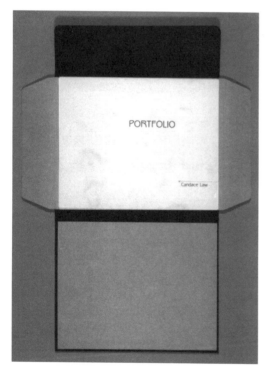

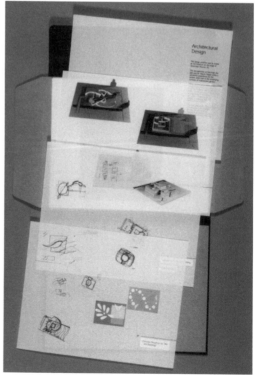

Rehearsal portfolio: plate portfolio with translucent pages of text in a four-leaf folder design.
Candace Law, Lawrence Technological University, Southfield, MI. 8 1/2" x 11"

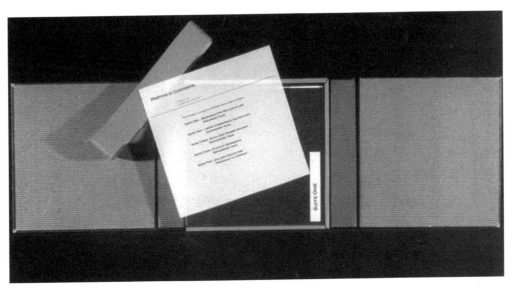

Rehearsal portfolio: a handmade portfolio box with bifold and trifold plate presentation.
Adam C. Pew, Lawrence Technological University, Southfield, MI. 8″ x 8″ x 2 1/2″

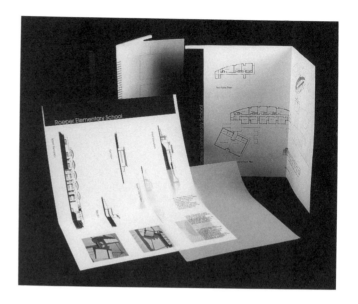

Rehearsal portfolio: unbound plates with
double- and multiple-folding pages. Each
plate is contained in a black, handcrafted
cardboard sleeve.
Matthew Coates, Lawrence Technological
University, Southfield, MI. 9″ x 12″

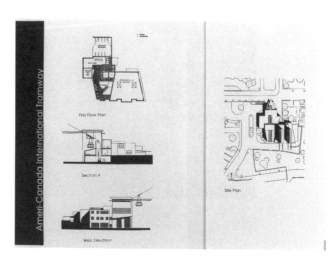

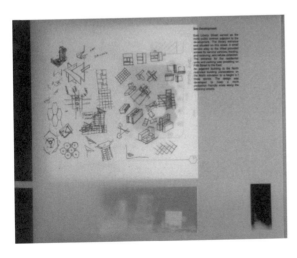

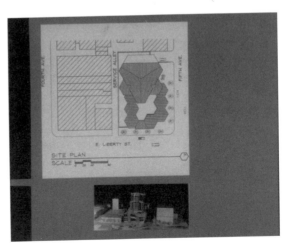

Rehearsal portfolio: individual project booklets in a handcrafted cover sleeve.
Karl Muegge, Lawrence Technological University, Southfield, MI. 9" x 12"

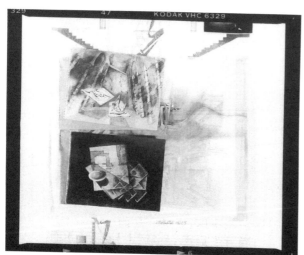

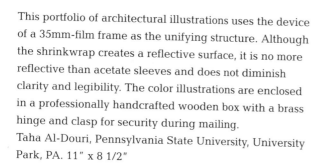

This portfolio of architectural illustrations uses the device of a 35mm-film frame as the unifying structure. Although the shrinkwrap creates a reflective surface, it is no more reflective than acetate sleeves and does not diminish clarity and legibility. The color illustrations are enclosed in a professionally handcrafted wooden box with a brass hinge and clasp for security during mailing.
Taha Al-Douri, Pennsylvania State University, University Park, PA. 11" x 8 1/2"

I believe the organization and layout of the portfolio itself is an indication of the student's capabilities as much as the work being presented. It is a work of art and, as such, it can demand everything from the simplest of tools to the most complex. Today, the technical tools available to most students can be both a powerful resource and a deterrent. Often, the tendency is to place too much importance on showcasing the capabilities of software at the expense of the work presented. Text, background, and line work often take on a role of dominance and do little to complement or highlight the design work. I like to see evidence that the experience of compiling the portfolio served as an opportunity for reflection at all stages of the design process.

Dr. Julie Rogers
Program Coordinator, Environmental Design
College of Architecture
Texas A&M University

with die-cut portions, tearsheet inserts and double-folded panels (see page 103). Such ambitious promotional brochures are naturally much more costly than individual designers and students can afford.

The final problem of portfolio design is achieving the best possible sequence of images for the most effective impact on the reviewer. Preliminary decisions about the ordering of material are made during the portfolio audit, but it is during the actual layout, while you are sizing and placing graphics on the page, that you discover how effectively the original plan will work, and make adjustments accordingly.

Two levels of sequencing need to be considered: the order and manner in which projects are presented and the transitions between different projects and the sequence of images within each project.

You may simply string projects one after the other, but one of the most common errors in portfolio design is the failure to make it clear where one project leaves off and another begins. The confusion occurs especially when different media—photographs, photostats, drawings, site plans—are used. Consider developing a standard divider page, like the chapter opening in a book, or some other visual signal of change, like a strong, well-designed heading. Another aid to the viewer is a "running" head identifying the project at the top or bottom of each page. You may know the content of your own work so well that the transitions seem clear. But

The storyboard is an invaluable tool for planning one's portfolio. It serves as the score for orchestrating the entire process. The creative designer develops many alternative strategies on the storyboard as reflections of the design process and a summary of personal design experiences. The discipline of rethinking the storyboard and the resourcefulness which an individual can bring to the planning process in its embryonic stage of development is essential. All of the attributes of a professional design education are reflected in the comprehensive organization of the portfolio and these are extremely valuable to an individual who holds the highest ideals for future practice".

Dr. Neville Clouten, Dean
College of Architecture and Design
Lawrence Technological University

without effective signposts, what is obviously a new project to you may seem like a new view of the previous project to someone not familiar with your work.

The number and arrangement of images on a page and on a series of pages controls the pace at which the reviewer is introduced to a visual problem and its solution. At the simplest level, you must always be conscious of where the reviewer's eye is being led, whether the reviewer's understanding of the your ideas is being helped or hindered, and whether the flow of ideas across the page prepares the reviewer for the next spread. And all this must be achieved while maintaining an overall consistent design for the entire presentation. Remember that in a bound portfolio the viewer's eye falls first on the right side of the right-hand page; all other things being equal, place your most important images there and use the left-hand page for secondary illustrations and text.

Sequences should have some logic or motivating force. For example, you might begin with simple pieces and work up to more complex images. Alternatively, move from exterior views of a structure to the interior, from close-ups to long views, from detail to overall, or the reverse. Start with a simple black-and-white sketch that lays out the problem, show developmental drawings, and end with the solution, rendered in a wider variety of graphic media. Search for a narrative principle conveyed in graphic terms, so the pages build on each other psychologically in the viewer's mind. To test your choices, try

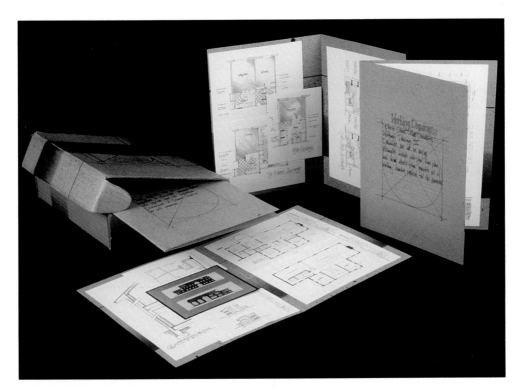

A corrugated cardboard box and 8 1/2″ x 11″ folders of speckled paper with
hand-lettered titles make simple but effective packaging for this interior design
student's application to graduate school.

Frederick Vasquez, Lawrence Technological University, Southfield, MI.

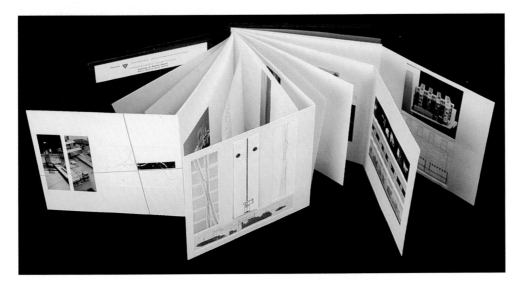

This handmade hard-back binder with bi- and tri-fold pages, sewn and glued
in place, holds a broad array of reprographic elements, including photostats,
cibachrome photographs, and other graphic arts materials.

Rachel Eberts, Parsons School of Design, New York, NY.

Graphics/Color Rendering

From the graduate portfolio of a landscape architecture student, this 8 1/2″ x 11″ page from a wire-bound portfolio shows strength in draftsmanship and sketching.

Elizabeth Saunders
Ohio State University
Columbus, OH.

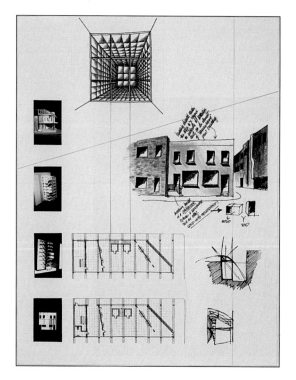

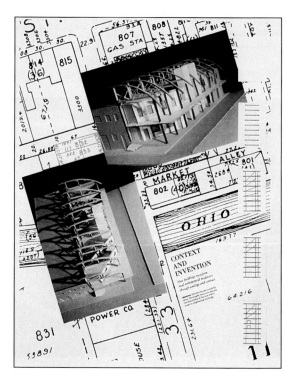

Submitted as part of a graduate program application, this portfolio conveys a dynamic vitality through the use of diagonals that interrupt its subtle underlying grid.

Carlos Brun, University of Miami, Coral Gables, FL.

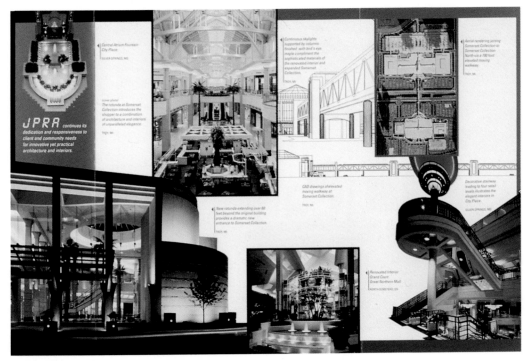

This is part of a promotion piece prepared by J. P. Ryan & Associates. The 9″ x 12″ brochure demonstrates sophisticated use of presentation tools: die-cuts, folding panels, inserts, and full-color printing.

James P. Ryan & Associates, Farmington Hills, MI.

These pieces from a student portfolio display strong computer skills; the renderings were done using AutoCAD and three-dimensional modelling programs.

Christopher Michael Garrison, Lawrence Technological University, Southfield, MI.

flipping quickly through the roughs, ignoring details and focusing on the progression of images, much as you would riffle through the pages of a cartoon flip book.

Building positive impressions quickly is your goal. You have to compress four or five separate projects into twenty to twenty-five pages, so you have no more than five or six pages to describe each project; hence the need for choosing strong, interrelated images, without any "filler." If your portfolio is too long, the reviewer won't look at it all; even if you are presenting the portfolio in person, the reviewer may cut off your presentation. In a half-hour or hour-long interview, only about half that time will be devoted to reviewing the portfolio, and its impact must be immediate.

Featured Portfolio

The work of Robert Zirkle is featured here to illustrate the element of sequence. His graduate portfolio was created as a graduation requirement for the master's program at Yale University School of Architecture. The design of the portfolio was intended to be predominantly visual. Robert referenced several architectural monographs as sources for ideas and inspiration and determined that the work should speak for itself.

The portfolio is bound like a book with a hard cover, with the outer surface wrapped in a high-grade book linen that provides a black matte surface with tactile appeal. A solid

A predominantly visual presentation of a master's thesis reflects a strong grasp of sequencing images, digital designs, and illustrations. Robert Zirkle, Yale University, New Haven, CT. 8" x 10 1/2"

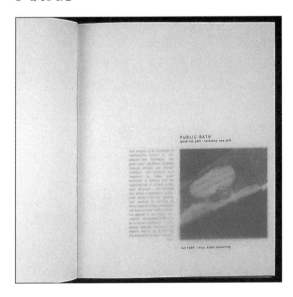

white background effectively emphasizes the graphic strength of the images. Each project is introduced with a mylar page and an offset black and white square image, with title information positioned directly above and below. Images were manipulated in Photoshop while the layout and text was organized using Illustrator.

The pages are printed on 11″ x 17″ Lumijet double-sided inkjet paper, allowing for two-page spreads with bleeds (no margins and borders). This technique drew attention to the content by utilizing the largest images possible. The images Zirkle presents are a combination of photographs of physical models, renderings of computer models, and architectural drawings. His designs were executed in a combination of InDesign, AutoCAD, Accurender, and Form-z. Some double-page spreads comprise one entire image, while other spreads reveal a large image on the right-hand page balanced against one or two smaller images placed on the left.

This portfolio is a beautiful example of a minimalist approach. The white space of the page is masterfully used to accentuate an asymmetrical layout design which relies completely on the quality of sharp, well-defined visual images to communicate its content.

Zirkle's portfolio was reviewed by Francisco Gonzalez-Pulido of Murphy/Jahn Inc., Architects in Chicago:

While the organization and form of Robert Zirkle's portfolio are very intriguing, and the concepts and ideas well expressed, it does not

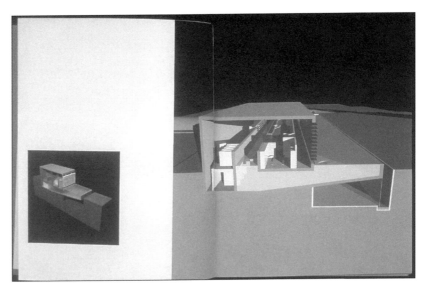

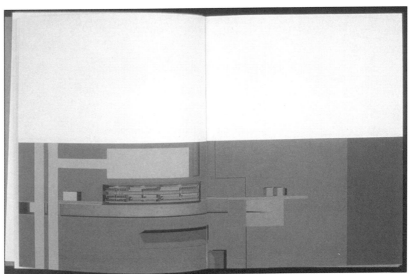

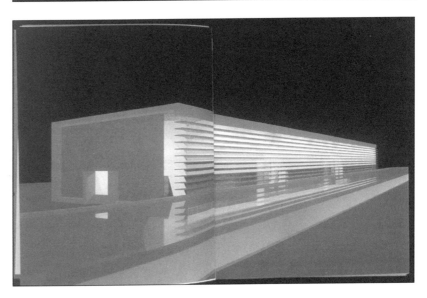

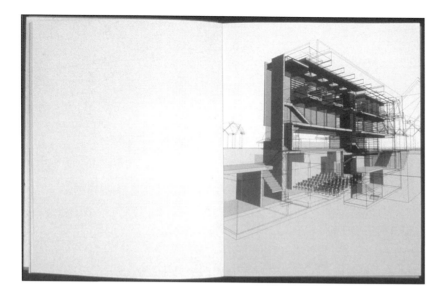

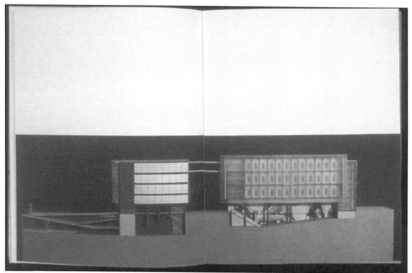

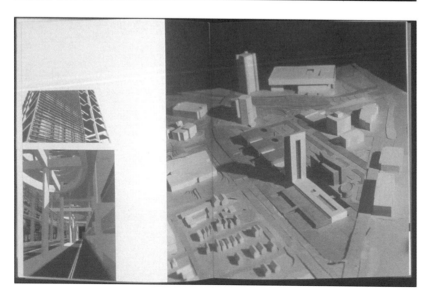

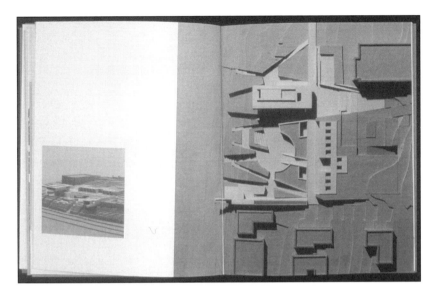

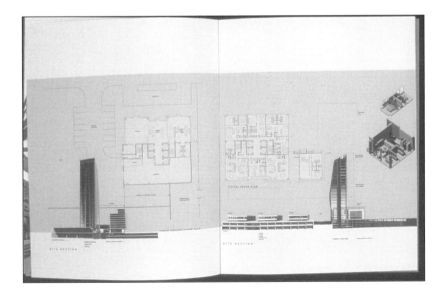

immediately make a definite impression. The format's precision and clarity make it a very intuitive presentation. At some point it becomes irrelevant where to begin reading the portfolio, because the layout's rationality allows for a total focus on its contents. The tension between the predictability of the organization and Zirkle's ability to strip down and present his design ideas in every image make a very strong impression over time. The absence of a table of contents conveys a sense of the portfolio as a compendium or montage—a book of design ideas. The graphic design is consistent and impeccable, but a little more information about the status and scope of the work presented would be helpful to understand the student's level of expertise. Both subtle and provocative, the portfolio builds the reader's interest gradually.

At first, the ambiguity created by the absence of text and a formal beginning is mystifying, but the idea of presenting every project as a visual narrative resolves that ambiguity. Defining an object with very consistent layers of visual information creates a seductive pathway to understanding its contents. The lack of background information is a strength that creates interest in learning more about the student. It triggers the need of talking to him in person about his work.

Sequence also implies progression in the design process from preliminary conceptual studies to fully rendered illustrations and models. J. W. Tisdale's pages show early drawings overlaid on the developed model (pages 84–85).

Clive Lonstein takes a somewhat bolder approach (opposite and page 68). His introductory pages are typographic, visually

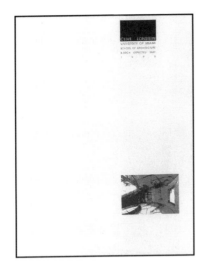

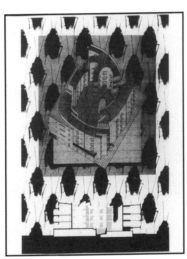

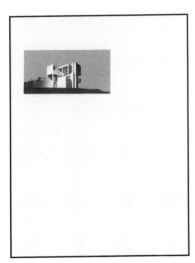
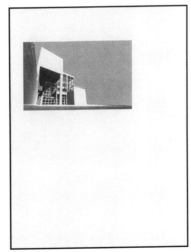

A varied and arresting sequence of text and images.
Clive Lonstein, University of Miami, Coral Gables, FL. 8 1/2″ x 11″

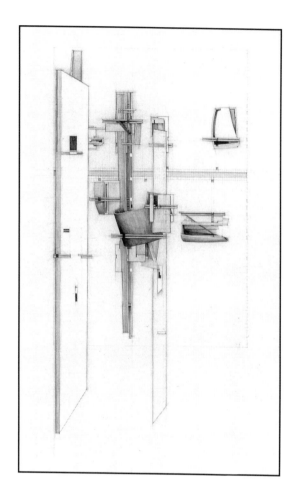

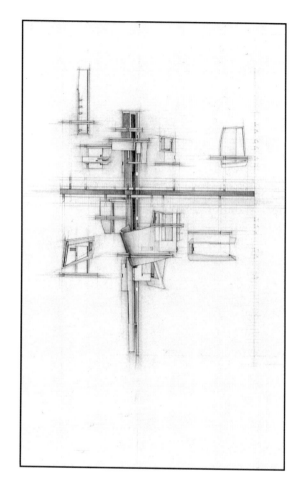

The exquisite plan and elevation views in
this portfolio are ranged in "chambers"
grouped in quadrants on opposite sides of
an axis. The careful application of gray
values and the abundant white space
around the drawings give them a jewel-
like character.
Thierry Landis, Pratt Institute, Brooklyn,
NY. 8" x 10" (top), 11 1/2 x 8" (right)

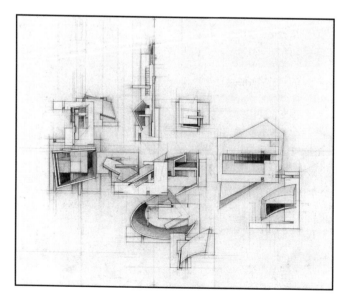

appealing, and easy to read. The illustrations that follow are a dramatic change of pace. A full-page self-portrait in the middle of the portfolio (not shown) signals the introduction to a sequence of architectural sketches centered in white space, all of which reveals the designer's strong drawing skills. Another dramatic transition with the sequence of computer-generated images that move from a small exterior view positioned at the top of the page through a progression of increasingly larger views of the interior design space, demonstrates sensitivity to the arts of animation and cinematography.

Thierry Landis's sequence of drawings (opposite), plan and elevation views of a living/working environment, was a project in twelve-tone drawing. Arranged in clustered chambers on opposite sides of an axis, with abundant white space, the drawings have a jewel-like character.

The portfolio of Tim Collett (page 114) is a good example of careful pacing. In order to separate one project from the next, Collett has grouped his projects in individual suites by delicately sewing together all the pages associated with each project, using a translucent paper cover and printed title.

John Maze's portfolio (page 115), with its regular alternation of text and graphics and varied images, presents a good solution to the problems of sequencing that confront the designer. Sequencing is as much a problem for the novelist or nonfiction writer as the designer, but the novelist can signal to the reader quite specifically in his prose when a

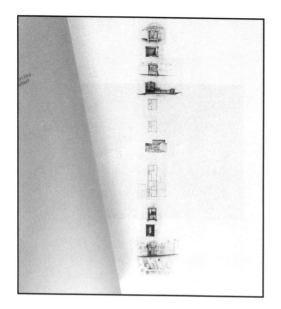

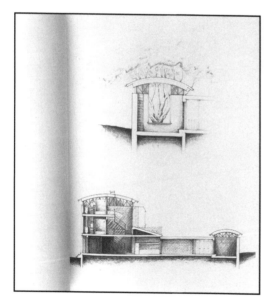

Another use of translucent overlays, in this case to introduce the sequence of images. Tim Collett, Technical University of Nova Scotia, Canada. 8 1/2" x 11"

scene is ending and what is likely to happen next. The graphic designer must accomplish the same thing with a series of visual images and a minimum of prose, and the conventions and emotional content of visual images are more ephemeral and less clearly defined than those of writing. Reactions to the effect of a particular graphic design are more varied. Still, seventy years of experience with the techniques of cinematography has taught us quite a bit about how sequences of visual images build their impact. Changes of scale, focusing in on a significant detail, changes of perspective, and varying the technique of presentation are all part of the process. Is there a logical and interesting flow to the work, or does something hold you up and stop you? It is difficult to lay out rules for sequencing because it is such an intuitive process, but each portfolio will either have an engaging sequence of images or it won't, and as you gain more and more experience you will be able to tell if you have succeeded fairly quickly.

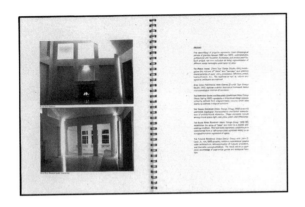

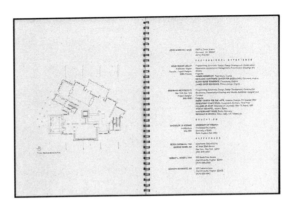

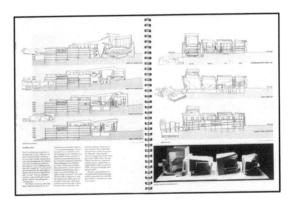

A professional's portfolio that packs a great deal of information in.
John Maze, Arizona State University, Tempe, AZ. 8 1/2″ x 11″

The home page and other pages on the Web site
of Frederick C. Gibson, San Francisco, CA.
8 1/2″ x 11″

4.
Digital Strategies:
Images and Text

All of the portfolios presented in this chapter are examples of work created with digital media. Now that you have carefully prepared a layout design, we will discuss all of the elements necessary to bring your work together in a digital format. In this chapter you will learn how to prepare the design content of your work for digital presentation by identifying images and text to be used, and how to create a digital template that corresponds to your storyboard using one of many software packages available. We will then discuss pasting, or inputting, the images and text into the template structure. When you achieve desired placement, you will scruti-

In our program of architecture at Southern Polytechnic State University, we see the digital portfolio as an extension of the process of design. We are developing a culture that makes seamless the customarily separate endeavors of research, process, design, and presentation. By approaching the project in all phases with digital documentation, we find a project's design can much more readily incorporate the process of design, and the presentation can clearly articulate what aspects of the process were most meaningful to the final design. The portfolio becomes essentially the presentation of the design, but with an important difference—the process is a visible, integrated portion of the design. With the "portfolio as design presentation" goal, we are able to more realistically portray the design processes involved in the solution. A practical benefit is that the portfolio, with its obvious professional benefits, becomes a product of the studio design effort.

C. Richard Cole, AIA, Professor
School of Architecture
Southern Polytechnic State University

nize the results and make necessary modifications to improve the portfolio's quality and visual impact.

The advantages of using electronic media in portfolio design and delivery include significant quality control, flexibility with graphic-design layout, ease of editing, time saved in exploring graphic alternatives, and instantaneous communication of the portfolio throughout the world. Digital technology has also made it possible for designers to easily produce multiple copies of their portfolios with slight variations for different purposes (e.g., job, school, or grant applications).

There are several ways to create images using a computer: (1) scan hand-drawn work (or photographs); (2) make images from scratch inside the computer; (3) capture images using a digital camera and transfer to the computer; and (4) use combinations of the above ways to create images. Once an image is in digital form, it can be flipped, rotated, enlarged, sharpened, or otherwise manipulated quickly and easily with far greater ease than with nondigital techniques.

The personal computer packaged with relatively inexpensive peripherals such as printers, scanners, modems, CD and DVD-ROM drives, graphic tablets, digital cameras, and page-layout and illustration software, has made desktop publishing a relatively accessible task, permitting individuals to produce finished, high-quality graphic work from a single computer work-

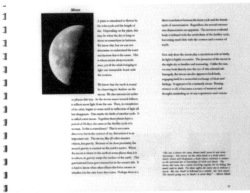

Cover design and sample pages from the Master of Architecture thesis presentation of Matthew Coates, University of Illinois, Champaign-Urbana, IL. 8 1/2" x 11"

station. Universities and design centers typically have such equipment available. Macintosh- and Windows-based software is becoming so intuitive that it enables the designer to work fluidly with visual form, space, and context.

A general rule to keep in mind about the computer is that it is important to understand the difference between what the computer can do and what the printer can do. One of the most frustrating aspects of computer graphics is the coordination between printer and computer. Sometimes the printed results do not appear the way you expect them to. This is why it is important to make test prints, as described later in the chapter.

As with any medium, it is important to quickly establish what the final presentation format will be so that you can guide your decisions throughout the process. If you are considering a large or small hard copy, you would either increase or limit your detail and resolution. If the final presentation is a 2-inch-wide image on a Web page, your decisions will be different than if you are making a video, and so forth.

The Master of Architecture thesis presentation of Matthew Coates is a traditional print portfolio packaged in a translucent vellum paper cover, the interior pages made using a computer. It demonstrates an effective relationship between word-processed text and visual imagery. Text paragraphs wrap or cradle the corners of the visuals throughout the layout, reflecting the thesis design concept of a birthing center.

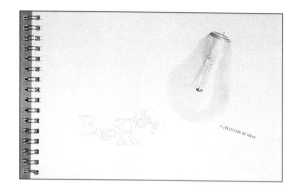

"Collection of Ideas"—the title the student gave to his portfolio—was created to demonstrate creative brainstorming and original design concept development.
Bryan S. Ridley, California Polytechnic State University, San Luis Obispo, CA. 5" x 8 3/4"

It is very important to plan, beginning with preproduction storyboards and mock-ups as described in previous chapters. Not only is the initial layout design fundamental to establishing the desired footprint, composition, and sequence of images and text, but it is essential when doing time-consuming computer renderings, so as not to render views you cannot use. It is also instrumental in directing the digital processes of media preparation, image manipulation, and printing.

Many powerful tools are available to the digital designer. The guidelines for planning a successful layout in traditional media also apply to digital portfolios. Once the storyboard is established, the graphic evidence (photos, drawings, and sketches, etc.) is converted to digital form.

The raw visual materials of CAD, photographs, models, and sketches were used to form a page layout in Bryan Ridley's portfolio entitled "Collection of Ideas." The work of Ridley, a student at California Polytechnic State University, demonstrates some of the basic layout possibilities that digital assistance affords. Linear elements and photographs, created in FreeHand and Photoshop, respectively, are used as introductory commentary to his projects. These pages utilize full-page bleeds, clever cropping, and an artistic composition that are realized in both the software packages.

Typically, source material can be either scanned on a flatbed scanner or captured with a digital camera. Because these images require a large amount of memory, it is best

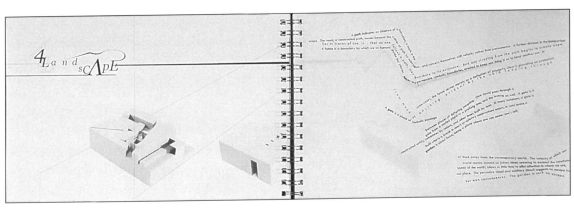

to store them on a Zip disk or a Jaz disk. Another option is to burn the images onto a CD. Since CDs can store up to 700 megabytes, they are especially appropriate and convenient for video or movie clips.

One useful trick you can use is to model your designs using a good three-dimensional modeling tool, such as 3DS Max. You can decide which views you want to capture by moving the camera and taking "snapshots" of the views you like. These can then be imported into Photoshop as two-dimensional images where their representation can be further enhanced or adjusted. Always be

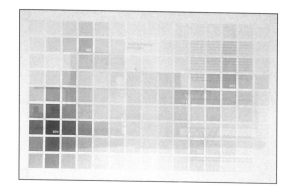

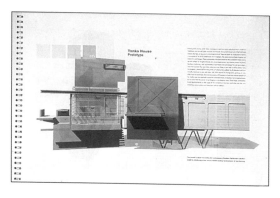

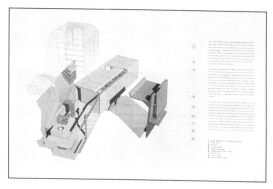

Skidmore, Owings, & Merrill's portfolio submission for a traveling fellowship specifies a 12-page limit and maximum page dimension of 11" x 17." Bryan S. Ridley, California Polytechnic State University, San Luis Obispo, CA. 11" x 17"

aware of your use of computer memory: try to do more with less. For example, make sure that all the lighting effects that take up a lot of memory and running power are actually visible in the final product. If the effects do not contribute to the current view, you should disable them to speed up the process.

A more comprehensive portfolio by Bryan Ridley demonstrates further layout strategies. The cover page is a simple array of colored squares varying in hue and saturation. It also serves as a table of contents, providing subtle cues to indicate a numeric order and a color theme for each project. Each project is, in turn, visually consistent with its respective color theme. The slight separation between the color blocks reveals another design element: the grid. This grid serves as the framework, providing the structure for developing the format of each page. The images presented were scanned and adjusted for size, contrast, and color in Photoshop. Many of the images are views of three-dimensional models, created using Form-z, with careful consideration of the application of color. The final page layout and layering of text was done using Macromedia FreeHand. To present images of varying transparency, the portfolio was printed on a commercial color laser printer with a combination of 6 mil polypropylene—heavy gauge plastic—brilliant white vellum, and opaque matte inkjet paper.

A good resolution for print material ranges from 150 to 300 dpi (dots per inch). This is usually sufficient to provide clear results. Resolutions of less than 150 dpi may result in

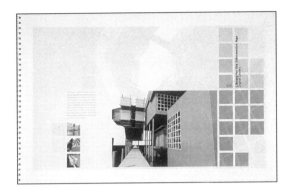

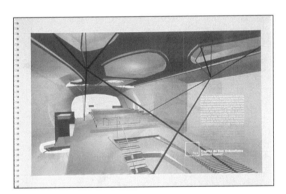

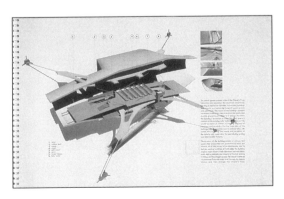

poor image quality; higher resolutions take up excessive disk space and do not noticeably enhance image quality. Some printers can only print files with a particular dpi, so it is preferable to know from the beginning how your portfolio will be output—that is, whether you will be using a professional service or an inkjet printer hooked up to your computer. To maintain consistency, select images of similar quality (color balance, sharpness, etc.) and scan all images at the same dpi. Adjust settings to provide for the best range of values and colors for an original document. Visual information is generally saved as TIFF files because they are high quality and have minimal compression, unlike JPEG files, which are compressed and degrade the quality of the image. This degradation is particularly noticeable after editing and repetitive operations. The JPEG file format, however, is appropriate for Web authoring because of the reduced image size. After the image has been converted to digital format, compare the consistency of the image on the monitor to the test prints and calibrate the monitor as necessary to ensure high-quality print material. Image-editing software provides directions on how to accomplish this for individual systems: it is different for every program, and the technology changes frequently. Once your monitor is calibrated, and your settings adjusted to compensate for any differences, you will have a better sense of any discrepancy between the two different media—the monitor and the hard copy.

Images can be enhanced and modified once they are scanned and stored in files. Not every scanner provides a perfect representation of the source material, but the color, contrast, sharpness, size/scale, and resolution can be adjusted digitally. Color correction generally includes modifications to hue, value, and chroma. Especially important is the range and balance of value contrast in original images scanned into the computer. Images lacking a clear range of light and dark will appear blurred and lose detail and visual interest. Images strong in contrast maintain their definition on the computer and in print. Sharpness refers to the texture or graininess of an image. Some control is offered through image-processing filters that sharpen or soften the texture of an image. (Sharpness is not the only goal: some very striking presentations can be made by combining low- and high-resolution images.) The size and scale of original images can be maintained or adjusted according to portfolio layout requirements. Similarly, the resolution or dpi can be modified to economize file space. File management, or the careful consolidation of file space, is an important part of mastering digital media. The goal is to be able to balance high-quality images with small file size. Remember, however, that once an image is scanned at a certain dpi, you can only lower its resolution (which makes it smaller). If you increase the dpi, the image will degrade.

The work of Paul Matelic and Julie Kim, partners of studiozONE, llc., are examples of

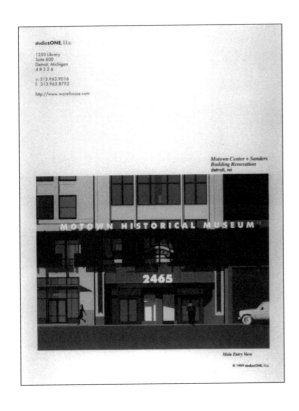

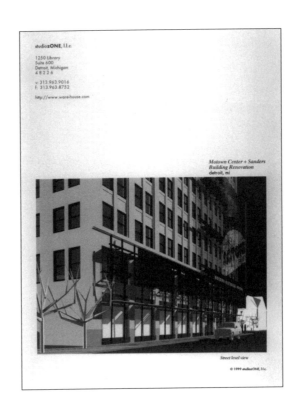

Images from a recent project, using a ray-traced AutoCAD image brought into Photoshop for additional modification, including the addition of figures, transparency, and lighting effects, for Motown Center + Sanders Building Renovation.
Paul Matelic and Julie Kim, studiozONE, llc., Detroit, MI. 8″x 10″

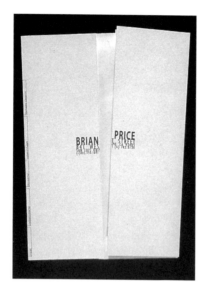

A mini-portfolio is useful for an introduction or resume, and a few sample projects.
Brian Price, California Polytechnic State University, San Luis Obispo, CA. 6″ x 8″

architectural illustration in which most elements have been redesigned and expanded through digital manipulation (page 125). Their work reflects the integration of technology and creativity at every level. By mingling computer illustration, photography and graphic design, they create a multilayered architectural design experience that envisions the future of the urban landscape.

The undergraduate portfolios created by Brian Price of California Polytechnic State University are examples of digital presentations in which architectural content and graphic design have been thoroughly integrated. A mini-portfolio or brochure containing a resume and sample projects is useful for introducing yourself to a prospective employer, and unfolds into a freestanding form. Price's larger, bound portfolio, useful for job interviews, includes project images and text printed on one side of the paper and formed into a double (inverse) French fold.

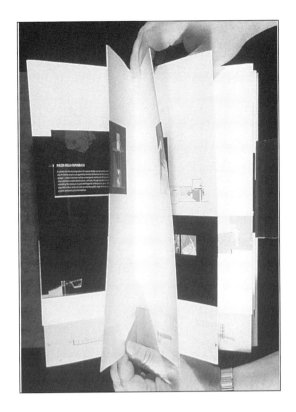

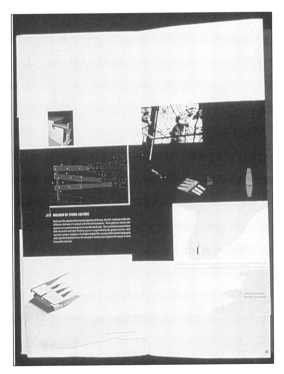

The use of a double French fold transforms a flat page into a multidimensional design presentation. Brian Price, California Polytechnic State University, San Luis Obispo, CA. 9″ x 12″

The integration of computer illustration, photography, and graphic design was created in Photoshop, FreeHand, and Form-z.

Test printing on the printer of choice at the early stages of image creation and manipulation is very important. Pages from the book and brochure by Price were produced on a Macintosh and test printed on an Epson Color Sylus 1270 printer. Many different imaging techniques can be used, yielding halftones (photographs), line art, and type in a seamless layout. Printers vary in density, clarity, and color. It is not uncommon for an image that looks brilliant on screen to appear muddy and/or yellowed in print. This can be corrected by manually calibrating your monitor to match the printer color range. Gamma adjustments can also affect the lightness, darkness, and color densities of certain hues. The age of print cartridges may also affect print quality. You can use different color settings when saving files: line art and black-and-white photos call for black-and-white settings, while CMYK is used for color files that will be printed and RGB is used for color files that will remain in digital format or be made into slides. Of course, digital technology is only as good as the available reproduction methods. High-end laser and dye-sublimation printers are now achieving a quality of reproduction that rivals traditional photolithography. Less expensive inkjet printers are another option. The best inkjet printers can yield a print quality up to 1440 dpi.

Featured Portfolio

The portfolio presentation by Claire Imatani received the Malcolm Reynolds Prize in Architecture at the University of California, Berkeley, and the American Institute of Architects Young Architect Award: Best Design Portfolio for 2001. Imatani's portfolio design reflects graduate school application restrictions and requirements that limit the number of pages and the size of the portfolio.

The portfolio is contained in an elegant black, laser-etched acrylic cover. A detail of the etching—a graphic formed at the intersection of two lines—is enhanced with an accent of crimson color, and establishes a thematic image which is carried throughout the rest of the portfolio.

Thick and thin colored lines in either crimson or yellow are used to organize information. A single vertical crimson bar—similar to those typically used to portray a timeline—serves as a datum to balance the horizontal text of the contents page. On the project pages, colored lines define areas on the page. Large areas typically contain photographic images of physical models or renderings of computer-generated models. Smaller areas contain fields of additional information such as a combination of diagrams, drawings, text, and images depicting other views or highlighting close-up details. Each field is framed by a white line which, in turn, connects linearly back to the colored datum.

The project introductory pages, however, contrast starkly to the pages previously

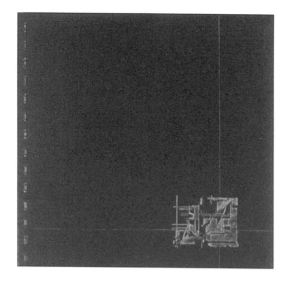 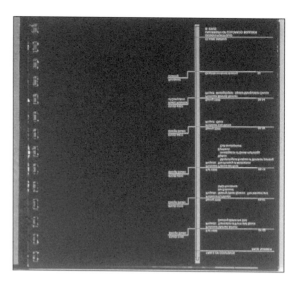

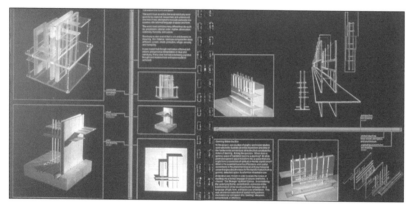

The contents of this portfolio were well documented on the computer,
allowing for a great variation of mock-ups in the graphic design process.
Claire Imatani, University of Colorado, Boulder, CO. 8″ x 8″

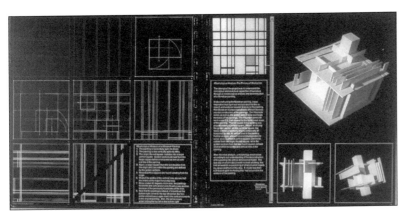

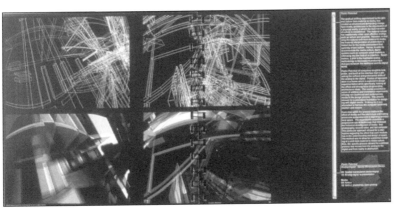

described: they are bold and colorless abstract images printed a white vellum, creating the effect of a reverse negative image. In addition, the page depicts simple intersecting black lines which allude to the primary portfolio structure and draw attention to the project title located at the intersection.

The selection and use of color is important in this portfolio. All of the project pages feature a black matte background allowing the images to stand out, while the white text serves as a great contrast. The crimson and yellow colored lines provide a visually linear progression of the information presented.

Imatani's portfolio is high in visual impact. The simple color palette is dramatic and creates a strong visual rhythm throughout the entire portfolio. It is successful not only in its visual consistency but in its visual manipulation of the fields of information for each project.

Peter Lynch, of the Cranbrook Academy of Art, offers the following advice on her portfolio design and presentation:

I review a few dozen portfolios every year as part of the graduate admissions process at Cranbrook. When I examine the portfolios, I look for clarity of thought—in the work and in its presentation. The portfolio is a means to an end. In my opinion, it should not call undue attention to itself, except insofar as it is an example of clarity, elegance, and good judgment. Instead of spending a lot of time in Photoshop, PageMaker, Quark, etc., a student should concentrate on refining, editing, and organizing projects, and on preparing simple and clear descriptions.

Oftentimes a portfolio is the only quick reference available for past design projects. Because it is a working document, it should be updated during each project. With the time pressures placed upon a professional design studio, there is never time to go back!

Scott A. Erdy, Associate
The Hillier Group
Princeton, New Jersey

Make sure to represent your work adequately; do not neglect basic information, like site plans, in favor of supplementary information, like perspectives. Clearly identify your specific contribution to collective projects. Do not lavish time and expense on elaborate graphics, fancy typefaces, unusual materials, or complex carrying cases and bindings. Many students have a strong temptation to overlay images from their projects—I think they do this to convey a sense of intellectual density, stylishness, and sophistication. Please resist, for your own good! Graphic design overload may once have been trendy, but it's now passé. To me, an excessive use of montaged and layered images usually suggests that the students do not know what is important and what is not. I wonder if they use graphic technique as camouflage. On the other hand, do make sure your printing is of high quality, and the images are high resolution.

Given this basic outlook, I feel that Claire Imatani's portfolio is carefully prepared but a bit overdone. It does successfully convey the most important message, however—that this student has many talents, and is passionate about her chosen subject. The use of black, the etched plastic cover, the graphic motif of the red bar, and the vellum pages are all details ultimately unimportant to me. It would have been better if she had chosen a more conventional format, which would have allowed her to reproduce her extremely detailed drawings on a larger scale. She could have surrounded them with more white space, which is less claustrophobic than a crowded black background. At the same time, I must commend her for the amplitude of the presentation: I look at her drawings and images and recognize her energy, sincerity, and freshness of spirit.

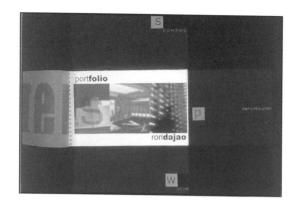

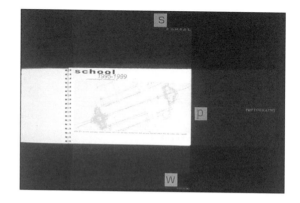

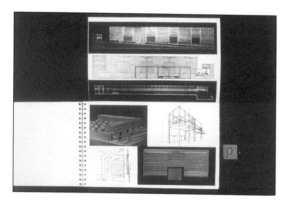

A sequence of unfolding panels creates a series
of flaps that, when opened together, form each
project presentation.
Rori Dajao, University of Virginia,
Charlottesville, VA. 4 1/2″ x 9″

One of the most distinct and often over-
looked influences on print quality is paper
choice. For all practical purposes, the document is only as good as the paper it is printed
on. Certain papers are better suited for different types of printing and there are countless
different types of paper on the market. Generally, paper varies in terms of fiber, size,
thickness, color, opacity, and finish. For high-
quality image printing, specially coated papers allow higher resolutions and more
accurate colors than uncoated papers and are
typically printed on one side only.

The portfolio created by Rori Dajao combines papers of varying opacity to achieve a
layered presentation of typographic design

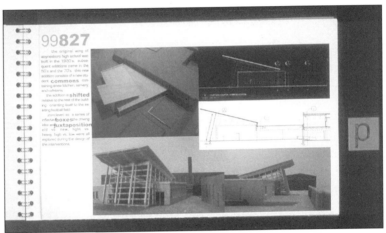

and architectural content. Cover stock, vellum, and coated opaque white printing papers open to the top, sides, and bottom to reveal the views of each design project. The portfolio was created with PageMaker, Photoshop, and Microstation, and printed with an Epson color laser printer.

Only after you have planned and test-printed all of the important aspects of image manipulation, size, color, and text, will you be ready to print the final pages of your portfolio. It is preferable to keep both the layout document and the images on the same disk, as the layout program will need to refer back to the images for good print quality. You now must decide whether to print the portfolio at a service bureau or use your

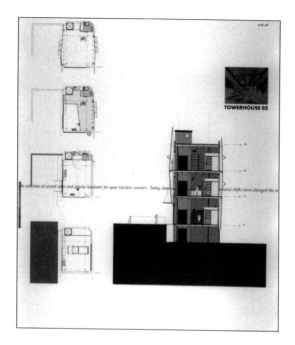

The work of Julie Kim reflects the integration of photography, typography, drafting, and illustration into elegant, open page layouts. Julie Kim, studiozONE, llc., Detroit, MI. 8″ x 8″

own printer. First, you should check to see whether your service bureau's printer offers you a better print size, paper quality, and/or reproduction quality. Service bureaus often have color laser printers, which are better than inkjet printers. Before you decide on the final print quality, you should review the format size of the portfolio. Printing at a service bureau is usually more expensive, unless you are making a lot of copies; if you print it yourself, you may have more flexibility with the format.

Software for creating and altering digital images is a new tool for architects and those in the allied fields of landscape design, interior architecture, and environmental and urban design. The work of Julie Kim, a partner of studiozONE, llc., reflects the integration of photography, typography, drafting, and illustration into elegant, creative page layouts. There are several key software packages for digital imaging in portfolio design.

Some of the most strategic packages include Adobe Photoshop, CorelDRAW, and Paint Shop Pro. All of these software packages allow the designer to easily change and correct digital images or to alter them to produce new images. The work of Gerardo Aponte (page 138) demonstrates photo manipulation in Photoshop with photographic distortion and text layered over visuals. Any image can be sharpened, cropped, expanded, reversed, inverted, or distorted. You can adjust contrast and brightness and blend, tint, lighten, and darken colors all in a matter of seconds. Images can also be layered by adjusting their respective transparencies. Text can be integrated with images and altered in equally varied ways. The many tools, filters, and effects of imaging software allow for an almost infinite number of variations on any given image. This range of possibilities is a great advantage of imaging software, but all the options can be confusing. A good rule of thumb is to know what you want to do before you start working on the computer. Even a relatively easy program like Photoshop can be a black hole of days and days spent tweaking the appearance of an image. More than saving time, such programs give you many choices to make, which sometimes means spending more time. Thus, you should avoid the trap of using the options offered without any esthetic goal just because they are there to be used. This is why it is so important to define what final product is desired.

With illustration programs such as Adobe Illustrator, Adobe Photoshop, Macromedia

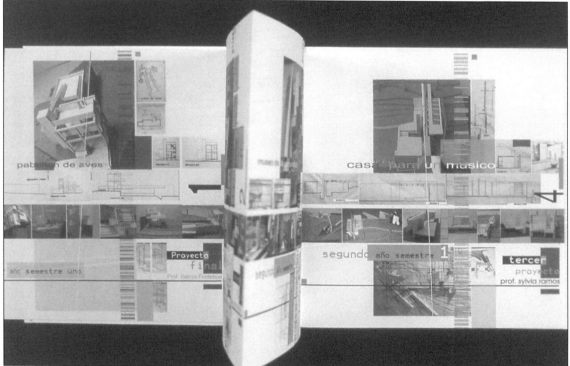

This portfolio design includes double-direction folded panels of five squares to the right and six squares to the left.
Gerardo Aponte, University of Puerto Rico, San Juan, Puerto Rico. 8″ x 8″

FreeHand, and Corel Painter, you can draw, sketch, place text, create and alter shapes, and import stored digital images. Pressure-sensitive digital pens used on graphic tablets simulate traditional drawing and painting media by responding to variations in pressure, angle, and edge. You can produce line art, watercolor, gouache, and other media, and use filters to change transparency, shading, or tinting. You can also add other effects such as pattern, pointillism, or embossing. Filters for lighting effects can simulate solar flare or give the appearance of multiple light sources of different colors, intensities, and angles.

With the latest versions of word processing programs such as Microsoft Word, Microsoft Works, and WordPerfect, to name a few, you can create text in any number of fonts and in multiple columns of varying width. Features such as Object Linking and Embedding (OLE) or media-import functions allow you to import almost any digital image into text columns; the text will automatically flow around or over it according to your specifications.

QuarkXPress and PageMaker by Adobe are best suited for combining images for multipage booklets, brochures, and portfolios. These widely used page-layout programs, among others, provide a broad array of layout possibilities. Text and images can be freely arranged on any page and resized, altered, or edited with ease. Consequently, this type of software is ideal for multipage documents like portfolios, which incorporate text with images and graphics. The programs also provide tools for shading and for creating graphics such as lines, shapes, and volumes. Remember that the goal of a portfolio is to communicate, specifically to "tell" about your work, and to do so clearly and convincingly.

When choosing digital tools, consider the following: (1) If the final output is to be hard copy, combine the strengths of different programs: for example, word processing is good with text and spelling; Photoshop is good with images (e.g., perspectives); AutoCAD and 3DS Max are good with architectural graphics (e.g., plans and sections). (2) If the final output is to be digital, Web, or CD, keep in mind that your work may be viewed by a variety of people with different levels of patience on a variety of computer terminals with different amounts of running power. Since your goal is to communicate, make sure that something is communicated easily and quickly. If your first image is so cumbersome that it takes several minutes before it can be seen, some people may give up and never see it. Start out with a screen page that is relatively simple, and only after that give viewers the option to see the more memory- and computer-power-intensive displays.

The use of computer-aided design, or CAD, is pervasive. This software enables the designer to create complex two-dimensional plans, elevations, and sections; software such as 3DS Max and Form-z are good for making three-dimensional models that can be altered, rotated to new perspectives, or even "entered" as if they were real structures viewed from different points of view. In many instances, these three-dimensional images replace the need for traditional model building, as the computer models can be constructed relatively quickly, can illustrate multiple design variations efficiently, and can be easily edited. "Snapshots" can be taken from any view and stored separately as image files. When frames of a three-dimensional computer model are rendered and saved as an animation file, they can be viewed in a consecutive manner, much like the frames of a film. Animated rendering can be done through 3DS Max, CINEMA 4D, and Maya. This gives the impression of moving through space. An alternative to rendering is to create a VRML file, in which you can "walk through" a space interactively. Among the more popular programs for this kind of work are Autodesk AutoCAD, Graphisoft Archi-CAD, Bentley Microstation, and Form-z.

Architectural Model Studios CD-ROM package
design by Jody Zoyes. Jody and Dean Zoyes,
Architectural Model Studios, Detroit, MI. 5″ x 5″

5.
Digital
Directions

Multimedia portfolios, which typically combine various formats such as CD- and DVD-ROM, Web pages, and animation and virtual reality applications, are a future possibility. CD and DVD-ROM drives are accessible for portfolio presentation. For example, Architectural Model Studios' CD-ROM and package design by Dean and Jody Zoyes includes a CD-ROM of office projects, sample prints from the CD-ROM, a description of office history on the inside flap, and a space for business cards.

CD and DVD disks are inexpensive and a single disk can house large volumes of data. The relatively small size is convenient for

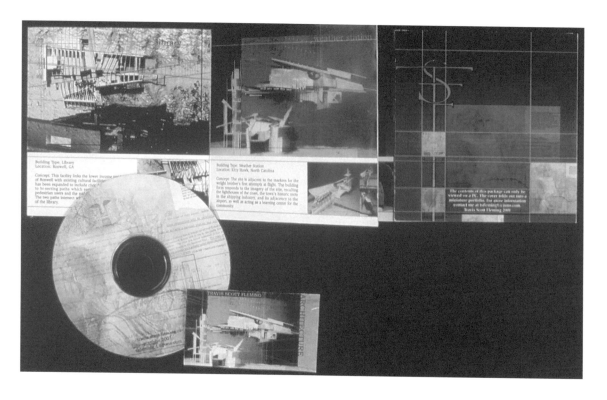

A CD-ROM portfolio includes an accordion fold inserted into the front of a jewel case.
Travis Scott Fleming, Southern Polytechnic State University, Marietta, GA. CD-ROM case, 5" x 5 1/2"

mailing to clients, copies are inexpensive to make, and the presentation can be in "real-time." Its economy also allows you to leave your work "on file" with a prospective employer for review at a later time.

Travis Scott Fleming's design for a CD-ROM portfolio of his work originated from the idea of music demo CDs and their use as introductory material for potential employers. The CD-ROM was created in Photoshop using model images, sketches and renderings, and photo montages that were then imported into Macromedia Flash. A physical portfolio—in the form of an accordion fold containing five projects with a brief description of each—was also designed to accompany the CD package. This fold was inserted into the front of a jewel case and a cover image was printed on CD labels, available at office supply stores.

There are two basic approaches to the planning and production strategy for CDs. The first consists of a choreographed, preset presentation, where the viewer experiences a total program from beginning to end without opportunity for interaction. The second choice, interactive viewer directed, requires the viewer to make choices that determine the order in which information is disseminated.

The choreographed CD-ROM presentation occurs in a linear format, which can be created with slide-show software such as Power-Point and Macromedia Director. The presenter has control over the timing, sequence, and cadence of information in the presentation. This software allows you to add animated text and graphics, make graphic transitions between slides, and create cinematographic effects and sound. It is relatively easy to learn how to use and offers opportunities for projecting the presentation on a wide screen in an auditorium. Create transitions that are fluid and consistent from frame to frame, and be sure the transitions are subtle and do not detract from the content. As with the physical portfolio, the digital portfolio should, above all, communicate.

Featured Portfolio

Georgia Institute of Technology student, Matt Vyverberg, created his portfolio in print form (and on CD-ROM) to submit as an entry to the Skidmore, Owings & Merrill Traveling

Fellowship Competition. The portfolio consists of four page elements: the cover, text, text with supportive graphics, and graphic statements. The cover is a composition of white and blue blocking, mottled textures, construction lines, and a grid element articulated to draw the eye around the page until it focuses on a die-cut window on which is printed Vyverberg's name in black and white.

The table of contents and descriptive pages utilize a technique similar to that of the cover, with a smaller graphic block set within a large white field containing the main headings and bounded by construction lines. Subtle construction lines call attention to the page layout. The visual and text organization ultimately work as a linear graphic element to make typography and visuals cohesive. The text is isolated and confined into "zones," and is either placed in the margin of the structure to indicate significance or within the body of the template for detailed descriptions.

Images that are used in conjunction with text are placed on the pages to emphasize the page structure of single and double columns. Care was taken to balance images and text so they do not compete for importance.

The pages that present the least structural complexity are those showcasing visual imagery. The images are a combination of architectural graphics, photographs, and three-dimensional renderings created in 3DS Vis, the light version of 3DS Max. Each page is limited to one or two images, which are

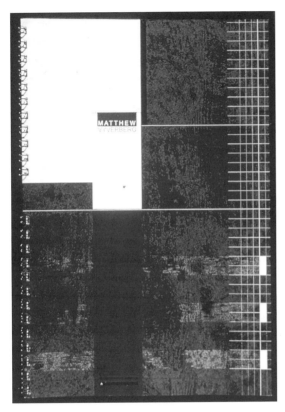

This custom-size print portfolio was created digitally and lends itself to a CD-ROM format. Matthew Vyverberg, Georgia Institute of Technology, Atlanta, GA. 10" x 15"

typically large so that they are easy to read and understand. The content of each image is visually rich and generates enough internal interest to engage the viewer in an otherwise minimalist composition. Many of the renderings are overlaid with varying transparency, a technique that simultaneously provides relief from and adherence to the basic orthogonal framework, resulting in a forced sense of spatial extension into the page and challenging the depth perception of the viewer.

Another element of interest is the two small graphic bars that sit at the bottom of every page. The thicker of the two bars remains stationary and helps to define the lower boundary of a "zone" with the blue graphic at the top and a margin to the left. The second narrow bar shifts position depending on the type of information communicated.

Matt Vyverberg's design strategies are clear and consistent without falling into the trap of repetition. The graphics are well executed with effective contrast and the images are visually captivating.

Tod Williams of Billie Tsien and Associates offered the following comments regarding Vyverberg's portfolio:

There is much to be admired in Matthew Vyverberg's portfolio. It indicates he is a serious and skilled student. I feel, however, that the portfolio is a bit over-produced and shields me from understanding him. The graphic strength tends to overwhelm the content. At the point when production challenges or overwhelms

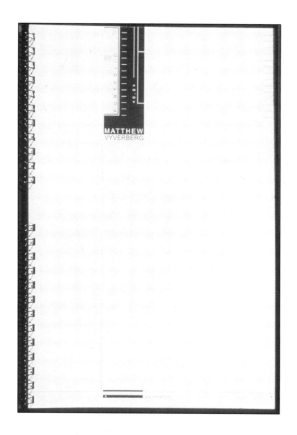

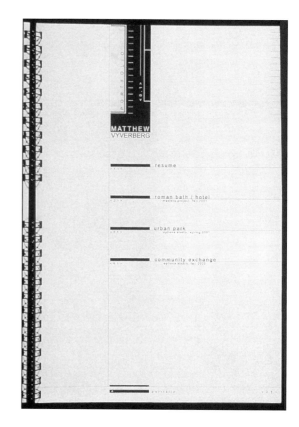

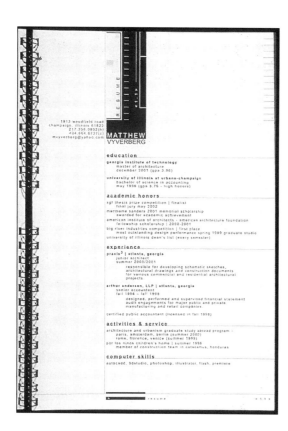

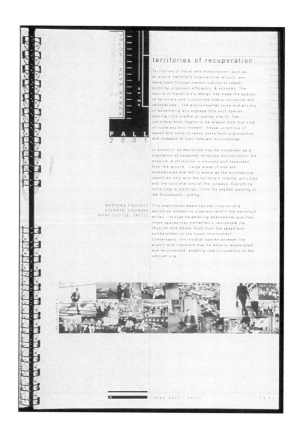

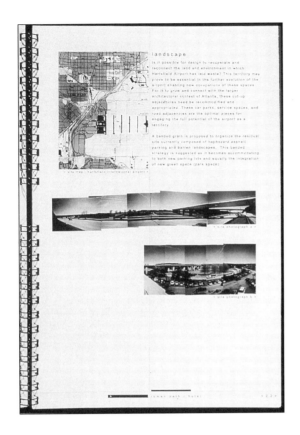

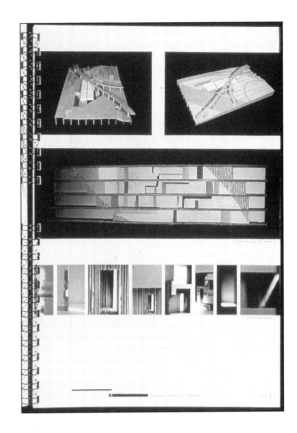

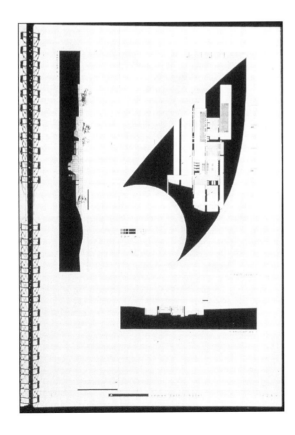

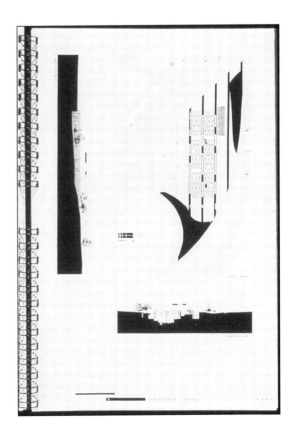

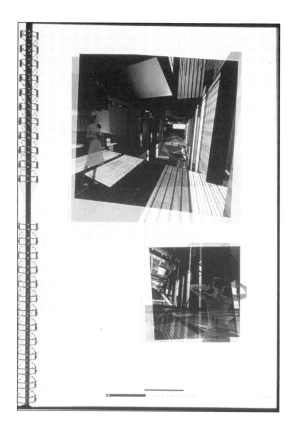

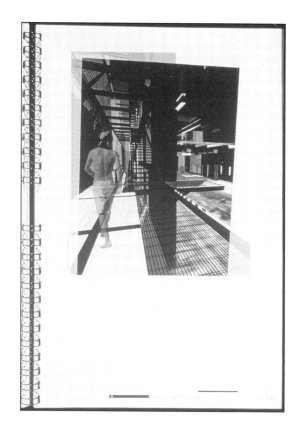

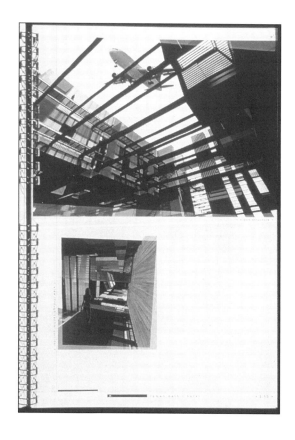

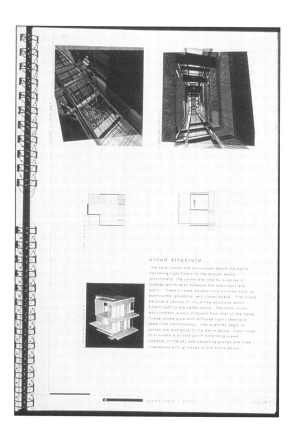

cloud structure

The hotel rooms are suspended above the baths becoming light filters to the spaces below. Structurally, the rooms are held by a series of trusses which span between the main concrete walls. These trusses equally hold utilities such as washrooms, plumbing, and closet space. The rooms become a canopy or cloud-like structure which filters light in the baths below. The hotel room environment is very different from that of the baths. These rooms glow with diffused light creating a jewel-like translucence. The qualities begin to soften the ambience of the baths below. Each room is provided a private porch extending views upwards of the sky and departing planes and view downwards with glimpses of the baths below.

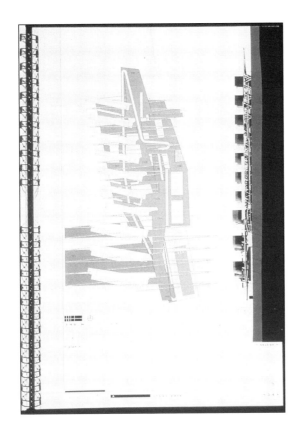

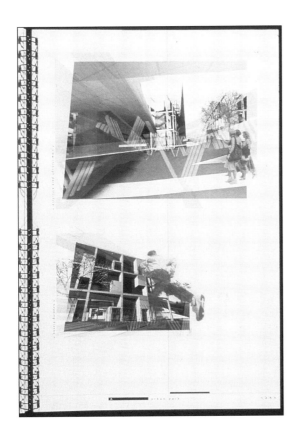

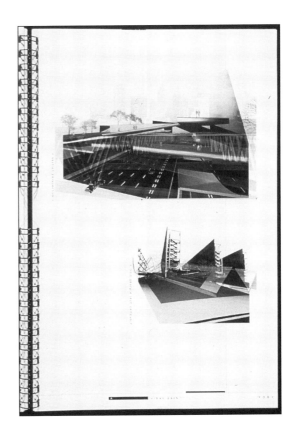

content, I question the way a candidate uses his or her time. It reminds me of a student who spent most of the year after school developing his college work, producing and ultimately binding it, much as a volume of Le Corbusier's *Oeuvre Complet*. He was a very good designer and student. Fellow students (including myself) were deeply impressed, but I had taken my original (not very brilliant) work, showed it directly to Richard Meier, and was given a job. The student with his fabulous book was never able to live up to the controlled brilliance of his portfolio. The story is not related to criticize Vyverberg but to remind students (and I must constantly remind myself) that one must strike a careful balance between expression and content. Relative to most, his portfolio is exceptional. Looking closely, the design work is very strong. Still, the computer-generated perspectives overwhelm the models and planning. My impression is that he might seek a larger commercial firm that would be more interested in him for his design and representational skills.

An interactive, viewer-directed CD-ROM presentation can occur in either a linear or nonlinear format (that is, the viewer can follow the linear organization or jump around from page to page). It is also created with slide-show software such as PowerPoint and Macromedia Director. Consisting of text, graphic information, and links to related slides, the presentation is controlled by the viewer, which enables him or her to focus upon areas of interest and bypass other areas. The viewer maneuvers through the presentation by selecting images, "hotspots," text, or buttons that link to additional images and information.

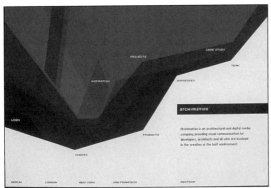

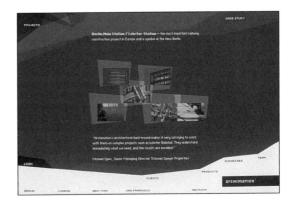

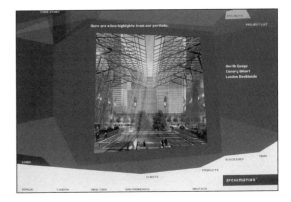

Digital renderings are contrasted against a
deep blue background for easy viewing and
high legibility.
Web site design: Katrin Middel; programming;
Jens Gehrken, Archimation, Berlin, Germany.

The structure for a Web portfolio is very
similar to the interactive, viewer-directed
method described above and differs only in
format. Instead of slides, Web pages display
text, graphics, and images that can link to
other pages to form a nonlinear presentation.
Sample portfolio pages from the Web site of
Archimation, a computer graphics and architectural imaging company headquartered in
Berlin, demonstrate an easy-to-use, content-
focused Web site. Thumbnail images of projects are shown collectively and the viewer is
invited to select them to view a larger, more
detailed version.

San Francisco architect Frederick Gibson presented his Web portfolio (page 116), by digitizing his work and digitally creating parts of it directly on the computer. His portfolio includes sample pages, architectural project designs, and even fly-throughs. He described his portfolio this way:

If you would like to experience the full depth of my professional portfolio in real time on the Internet's World Wide Web, please jump to http://www.gibson-design.com. One of the fascinating aspects of publishing on the Web is the ability to enrich and expand content with no concerns for print costs. The only limitation is time itself. I now have most of my portfolio itself, including photos, images, plans, sketches, construction photos, writings, and additional VRML (Virtual Reality Modeling Language), on the Web. My current vision is to use the World Wide Web as the complete archive of my past and current work with as much detail as the visitor would like to see throughout my career. An even more fascinating development on the WWW is the arrival of VRML. With VRML a visitor can 'virtually' walk and fly through a computer-generated three-dimensional environment. Although not as good as an actual site visit, VRML lets anyone on the Web explore the environments I design—an incredibly powerful way to experience my design portfolio.

Rossetti Architects in Birmingham, Michigan, designed a corporate Web site that demonstrates an easy-to-navigate portfolio of general information about the firm. The main page provides information about the company and its philosophy and mission, and the portfolio of office projects is subdivided into

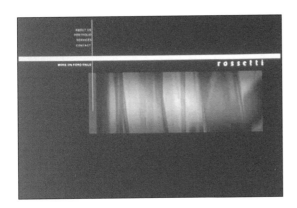

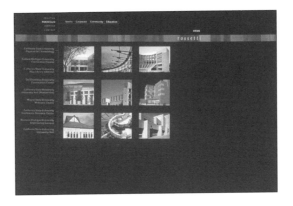

Rossetti Architects' Web site portfolio is organized around a predominantly visual presentation of design commissions.
Rossetti Architects, Birmingham, MI.

four categories: sports, corporate, community, and education. By moving the cursor, project images change from black and white to color, inviting you to click and view a larger, more detailed image with a text description of the design project and program.

When preparing images for Web applications, the goal is to keep image file size as small as possible by reducing resolution and limiting color range and values. This is common for the GIF file format utilized by most web pages. Typical images for Web publishing are created with a resolution of not more than 72 dpi because that is the resolution of the monitor. (If the image never leaves the computer screen, there is no need for higher resolution.) Web pages can be created with Microsoft FrontPage, Adobe PageMill, PowerPoint, eZediaMX, Anark Studio, and several other inexpensive programs. Putting your portfolio on the Internet makes it universally and instantaneously accessible and gives you the opportunity to receive a positive and/or critical response. However, it is important to realize that the medium is dictating new organization methods for how you present your work—the screen pages are no longer equivalent the way those in a physical portfolio were, but they need to remain graphically consistent to work.

The Web also allows you to link your Web page to related information, which helps to situate your work within a broader context of your choosing. More and more professional organizations, corporations, and individuals are establishing Web sites. Many Web sites offer "virtual portfolios"—a multitude of pictures and architectural plans from buildings around the world. Many universities maintain their own servers and offer Internet connections to their students as an integral part of program studies. If you have a computer and a modem, the Internet is certainly worth exploring. Go to one of the Web's popular search engines, such as Yahoo, WebCrawler, AltaVista, Netscape, Excite, Infoseek, to name only a few, and type in "architecture." You can find a great deal of career information, job listings, grant applications, announcements of competitions, and even a collection of images providing a mini-history of Renaissance architecture.

The information available on the Internet is growing in leaps and bounds. Here are a few Web sites, current at the time of writing (but addresses date notoriously quickly on the Web) that you may find of interest:

Rendering and Visualization

http://www.archimation.com
http://www.architechnology.com
http://www.imadjinn-cgi.com

http://www.bondystudio.com/DigRender/Dig
RenderHome.htm

Architecture Web Portfolios

http://www.geocities.com/CollegePark/3176
http://www.geocities.com/arqitecto
http://www.inbarbarak.com
http://www.ergoarchitecture.com/Portfolio
http://www.burthill.com/main_nav/main_nav.
html
http://www.payette.com
http://www.machado-silvetti.com
http://www.rossetti.com/flash.html
http://www.mmaarchitects.com

Commercial Products

http://imaginaryforces.com/index_flash.htm
http://www.lookandfeel.com
http://www.juxtinteractive.com
http://www.fahrenheit.com
http://www.virtual-planit.com
http://g.skydesign.com/flashOK.html
http://ap.nike.com/ap/presto/index_popup.html

Association of Collegiate Schools of Architecture
www.acsa-arch.org

Virtual Reality

http://www.skyscraper-digital.com
http://www.usa.cyber-image.com
http://www.schofields.com/the_edge/vr/vr_port-
folio_construction.htm
http://www.kinetichorizons.com/Pages/Asilomar
VR.htm
http://www.3dgallery.com
http://www.stevemiller.com/vrstudiotour/studio.
htm
http://www-vrl.umich.edu/projects.html

http://archive.ncsa.uiuc.edu/VR/VR/VRHome
  Page.html
http://www.dunearchitecture.com/vr/vrblade/
  vrblade2.htm
http://bruno.postle.net/world_of_vrml_tent_
  architecture
http://www.artotal.com/multi/mul3d.htm

Animating images as they come up for
viewing on the screen and virtual reality —
moving through three-dimensional models—
can be incorporated into Web-page and CD
and DVD presentation formats. Many of the
three-dimensional imaging software programs
described earlier are capable of creating animated graphics.

Animation can be created in two and three
dimensions. Two-dimensional animation can
be simple animated text, where letters "spin"
in place or "zoom" in from the sides of the
screen. Built into PowerPoint and Macromedia Director are limited animation options for
logos and adding the effects of movement to
two-dimensional shapes. More sophisticated
imagery and animation would typically be
created in other programs such as Macromedia Flash.

The interactive Web portfolio (www.geoci-
ties.com/CollegePark/3176/) created by
Steven Valenta, undergraduate architectural
intern at HKS, Inc., in Dallas, was created to
showcase his work for employment interviews. The design, using Photoshop and
Macromedia Flash, demonstrates basic animation and presents a combination of his
artwork, architectural renderings, and digital
imaging. On his home page, as you move the

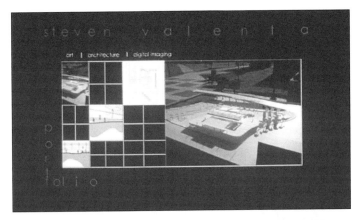

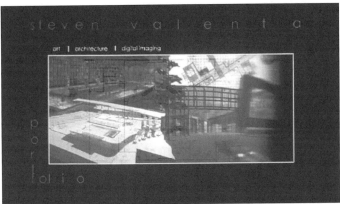

Steve Valenta's architectural design Web portfolio offers introductory pages of interactive sequences and basic animation to pique the viewer's curiosity. Steve Valenta, Texas Tech University, Lubbock, TX.

cursor from the category title of art to architecture, the image scrolls from right to left and reveals an architectural rendering. Flash software was used to create this effect. Then, as you move your cursor from architecture to digital imaging, the image scrolls again to reveal a computer rendered image. Valenta provides a list of specific projects for you to select and view.

Some choreographed presentations consist of nothing but animation. Basic three-dimensional animation entails a modeling process and the creation of geometric volumes, which can be done with any modeling software. Then physical, material properties (color, light, and texture) can be applied to the form. Animation can make volumes or forms appear to move through space or simulate a camera's movement (from the viewer's point of view) through volumes and space. CAD programs (AutoCAD, ArchiCAD, and Microstation) and graphic programs 3DS Max, CINEMA 4D, and Maya) are appropriate for three-dimensional rendering and animation. There also are several other inexpensive software packages, such as Form-z and Rhino, capable of modeling and rendering. This software can save models in VRML format, or Virtual Reality Modeling Language, which is a descriptive language that allows 3D geometry to be presented in a compact way. VRML is universal in that it works across platforms, including PC, MAC, and Unix workstations. Virtual reality models can be viewed on a VRML viewer on the Internet and can also be viewed with special glasses or in a CAVE (Computer Animation Video Enhanced system). The advantage of VRML is that a design idea can be experienced in a fully navigable, user-controlled environment. User control is provided through two modes: observation and navigation. In observation mode the user can spin the model around any axis of rotation as if observing an object in space. In navigation mode the user can

Donna Cox and Bob Patterson, professors of advanced computing at the University of Illinois, stand inside the CAVE observing a digital three-dimensional display of animation.
National Center for Supercomputing Applications, University of Illinois, Urbana-Champaign, IL.

move freely around and through the model
as if he or she were walking or flying.

The pages of Leonard Temko and Kristen
Gibbs demonstrate how, with a VRML
viewer, a visitor can virtually "walk" or "fly"
through a computer-generated three-dimensional study model (pages 162–163). The two
views of Le Corbusier's Villa Savoye House
were created by Temko and Gibbs, Master of
Architecture students at the University of
Michigan, in a VRML course at the
University of Michigan. In the Villa Savoye
model, navigation is offered by the textual
components, while the Schroder House
model uses graphics as navigational tools.

The nontraditional portfolio provides the
means for presenting two- and three-dimensional content in real time presentations.
Today, firms can look at current portfolios as
well as in-progress studio work to find
prospective employees. Computer-assisted
design critique can occur anywhere, any-
time, when the individuals in classes are
connected. At the Harvard Graduate School
of Design, students work with visiting professors who lecture at the university and offer
critical opinions and design dialogue online
once a week. The Design Studio of the
Future, a graduate architectural design studio at M.I.T., took place entirely on-line in
communication with five affiliated international universities. Students shared a data-
base as well as wide-ranging activities,
including final project review projected live
from all the participating universities at the
same time.

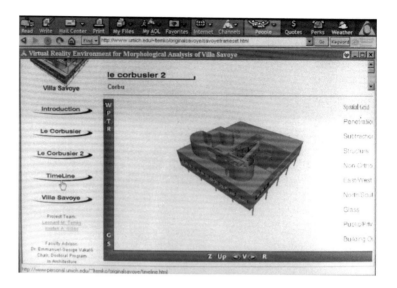

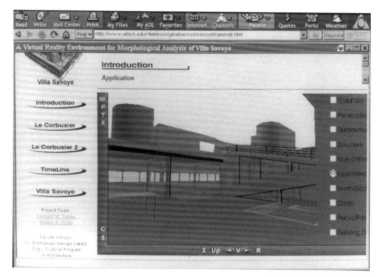

Web pages using VRML demonstrate how a visitor can interact with a computer-generated three-dimensional study model. The two views of Villa Savoye were created by Leonard Temko, doctoral student, and Kristen Gibbs, Master of Architecture, in a course under the direction of Dr. Klaus-Peter Beier, professor of naval architecture, Dr. Emmanuel George Vakalo, architecture faculty advisor, and Samir S. Emdanat, doctoral student of architecture and graduate teaching assistant, Taubman School of Architecture and Urban Planning, University of Michigan, Ann Arbor, MI. 8 1/2″ x 11″

Keep this thought in mind when considering nontraditional digital portfolios: a successful end result requires a strong visual foundation of design sensitivities coupled with equally strong technical ability. The successful presentation of your design evidence in digital format is a product of imagination, skill, and experimentation. Imagination and technical skill notwithstanding, however, digital technology is still in its infancy, at least concerning the reproduction of images, especially such graphics as plans, sections, and

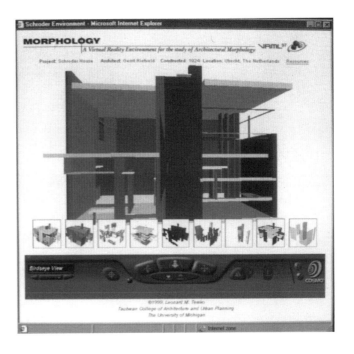

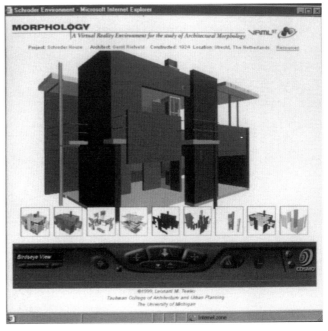

elevations. To get the best results in your portfolio, it is necessary to combine a variety of the tools available.

Many professionals prefer to see actual printed pieces of your work, even if a computer disk is included. Not only is a physical portfolio faster and more convenient to view, but it is the natural thing to bring in a face-to-face interview. There are other limitations to digital portfolios as well, including screen size, problems in software compatibility from office to office, and the effort of reading on a monitor. So think of the computer as a tool and an aid for producing flat, graphic designs of the traditional type. Eventually, the digital portfolio will become fully accepted, but for now a "physical" record of your work is still preferable to a virtual record.

An additional concern regarding portfolios disseminated on the Web is plagiarism. Portfolios on the Web reach a wide, anonymous audience, which means your designs can be copied without your knowledge. For this reason, many designers use the Web to showcase drawings and other images that don't reveal specific, technical information about their designs. If your Web portfolio attracts prospective clients or employers, you can then show them the more detailed examples of your work. This way you will have a better understanding of who knows your design secrets and who doesn't.

Margo Hutcheson, career coordinator for the College of Design at Iowa State University, conducted a small research project in which thirty architecture firms were e-mailed the following message: "I am working with a student who is interested in presenting a Web page portfolio rather than the traditional print portfolio during a job search. What are your thoughts on this?" The individual architecture firms' responses provide useful insight into this dynamic and evolving medium of presentation.

- A Web-based portfolio is a good way to find opportunities for job interviews. It will soon be the choice of many firms to review potential employees.

- Following the submission of a resume, an on-line portfolio serves as a useful intermediate step to explore our interest in a candidate's work and determine if an invitation to interview with us is the next step.

- The use of an on-line or CD-ROM portfolio provides the chance to see their work before setting up an interview, especially when discussing a candidate at a long distance from our office.

- Candidates who interview with our office are required to show a print portfolio whether they have electronic background or not.

- AutoCAD experience is absolutely necessary to demonstrate in a portfolio interview in our office.

- We suggest that a paper resume always be submitted with or without reference to a Web site.

- Our suggestions to prospective candidates include the following steps: prepare a resume, one page, clear yet graphically interesting, that can be mailed, faxed, and e-mailed as an attachment; include this on the Web page with Web site address; prepare two cover letters—one for mail or fax and the other for e-mail; prepare a Web site portfolio with links to all important aspects of your information; and prepare a print portfolio to take with you to the office interview.

- A print portfolio is expected. We feel the resume is the most important aspect of the application and without one we will not review a candidate's work. We do not have time to review either electronic or video presentations. A well-written cover letter and resume tell us all we need to know if we are interested in pursuing a candidate further for an interview.

The general response can be summarized: print portfolios are still an essential element of an architecture job search and are preferred in interviews. Web portfolios are an accepted method of introduction, especially when conducting a long-distance job search. In a way, Web pages function like the samples of work you traditionally might send with your cover letter and resume before submitting your full portfolio, to pique their interest. The commentary supports the role of the traditional print portfolio but also recognizes the growing interest in digital portfolio, especially in the early and less formal stages of the job search. These comments, however, also underscore the need for well-written documents to introduce, accompany, and integrate with a well-designed print portfolio. Stephen A. Kliment's book, *Writing for Design Professionals*, offers a wealth of advice on writing successful proposals, letters, brochures, portfolios, reports, presentations, and job applications. An ideal companion to this book, it provides instruction for the organization of good written communication to complement the visual research and design work necessary for unified visual organization in the portfolio, a combination that's hard to beat.

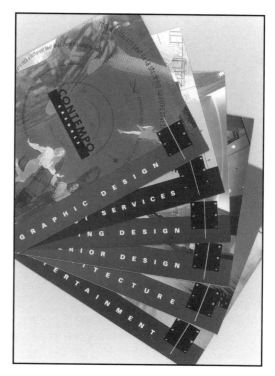

This professional portfolio from a design office contains individual, interchangeable pages showing the firm's projects. Many design firms use this kind of modular system, which allows them to include a selection of relevant pieces in a portfolio submitted for a particular job. Barry Ridge Graphic Design, Westlake Village, CA. 6″ x 9″

Another office brochure system with double-folded pieces selected to suit individual clients. SDI-HTI, New York, NY. 8 1/2″ x 11″

6.
A Portfolio
of Portfolios

Believing in the effectiveness of learning by example, I present in this chapter a variety of portfolios that embody novel or interesting solutions to questions of page structure, image presentation, and sequencing. You may find here a solution to your own design problem, or you may simply note a style or method to keep in mind for the future. In addition to looking at other people's portfolios, remember to stay abreast of design trends by making frequent trips to the library, reading contemporary journals, and talking to colleagues.

There are no rules set in concrete for portfolio design. You should cultivate an apprecia-

A black background gives dramatic contrast to a collage from a plate portfolio.
Jillian V. Lustig, Art Center College of Design, Pasadena, CA. 10″ x 13″

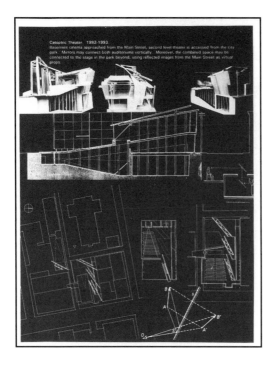

Pages that incorporate intriguing collages and photographs for dramatic impact.
Mark Morris, The Ohio State University, Columbus, OH. 8 1/2" x 11"

tion for contemporary imagery found in broadcast media, on-line Web sites, communication arts, and contemporary journals, and research into the discipline of typography and graphic design. The standards set by every portfolio shown here, and every guideline and caution detailed in the preceding pages, can be overturned if you feel compelled to do so by the nature of the material you are presenting. That is exactly how new ideas become old principles. But relatively inexperienced designers should proceed cautiously. Originality is important, but trying too hard to be original often leads the inexperienced designer away from commonly accepted principles of communication, and if you cannot make your ideas clear to other individuals, your originality will be applied to no purpose. There is enormous scope in portfolio design for original ideas, and reviewers will appreciate a bold leap of imagination, but they will also be looking for creativity tempered by a mature and realistic outlook. Never forget that most professional offices undertake projects as a team, and you will want to demonstrate that your boldness is not arrogance, that you possess discipline, and that you can function as a team player.

No matter how good your portfolio is, it will inevitably mean different things to different people. A design firm will react differently to your work than would an architectural engineering firm, a planning office, or a graduate school review panel. This is why it is so

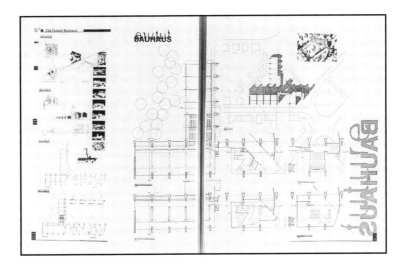

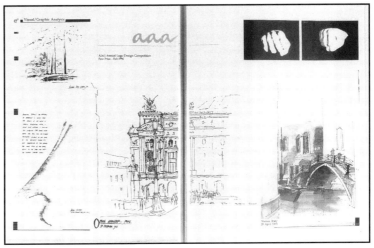

These layouts make excellent use
of double-page spreads to give
the drawings enough room for the
fine qualities of line and shade to
be seen.
Jesse Wu, University of Illinois,
Champaign-Urbana, IL.
8 1/2" x 11"

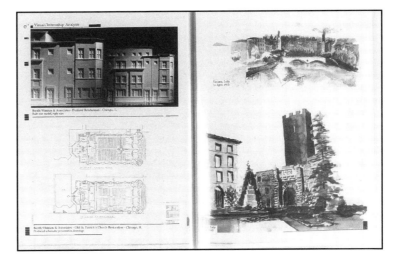

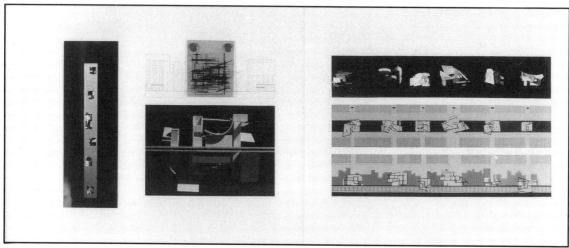

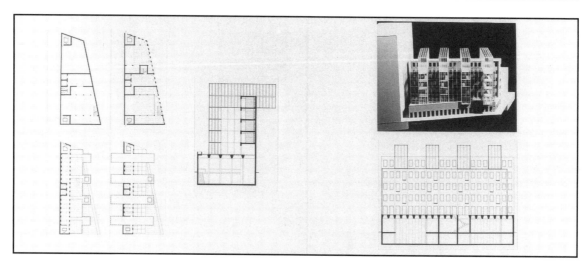

important to research the type of company you are planning to interview with, and if possible, to gear your presentation toward their interests. It's a good idea to let someone else review your finished portfolio before presenting it to a prospective employer. You want to know if something in your portfolio doesn't make sense or lacks an adequate explanation. Go over your portfolio yourself as objectively as possible, reviewing every element and how it works in conjunction with other elements. Ask yourself these basic questions: Is the portfolio well organized? Does it clearly illustrate your strengths and technical abilities as a designer? Does it show how your ideas develop and how you solve problems? Does it present a focused vision? Review the overall layout, the photography, the typography, and the reproduction methods. Are the pages in mint condition or have they become dog-eared after frequent reviews? Are the images presented sharply and clearly, with adequate contrast? Are the projects included up to date, reflecting your best and most recent work? Do the views of your work make sense, and do subsequent pages expand upon and make the previous pages clearer? Is the photography sharp and clear, and is the text legible? Will the reviewer understand the material without having you present to explain the portfolio?

Once your portfolio has won you an interview, what can you expect? A typical interview lasts a half-hour or more, and is normally conducted by a member of the faculty or administration or, in a professional

Hinged pages constructed from cardstock in a handcrafted case covered in black canvas by a book bindery.
Rachael Eberts, Parsons School of Design, New York, NY. 11" x 8 1/2"

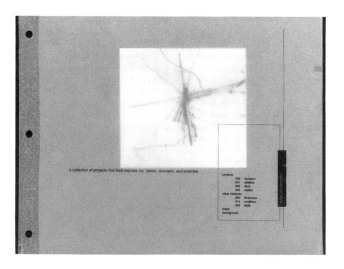

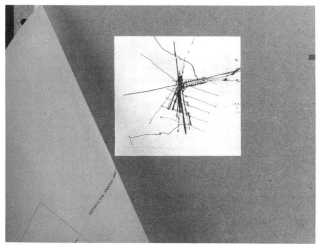

Overlays, ample text, and clear drawings,
mounted on textured paper.
Paul John Boulifard, North Carolina State
University, Raleigh, NC. 11″ x 8 1/2″

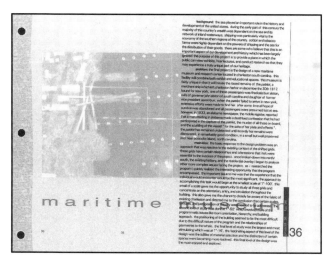

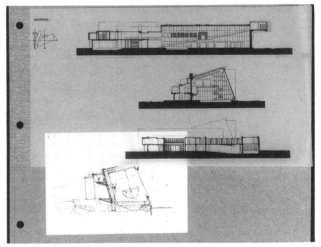

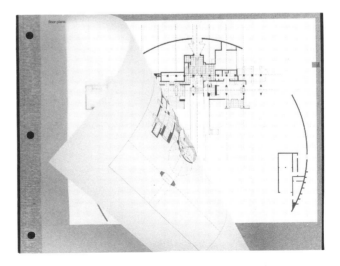

office, by a member of the design team, a partner, project manager, or personnel officer. You will be asked questions about your education, your previous employment and the projects you have completed, as well as, perhaps, a number of personal questions about your goals. Not everything the interviewer wants to know may be formally solicited through a question, but in general conversation you will reveal much about your personal interests and goals. Almost certainly, you will be asked why you chose your field of study and how you see yourself fitting into the school or firm. Know your portfolio and the projects in it well, and be prepared to talk about them. Learn from the experience if the reviewer is confused about some aspect of your presentation, and fix the problem before your next interview.

It is also important to come to the interview with some carefully prepared questions of your own. Unless you demonstrate interest and curiosity about the company and your position within it, the interview is not likely to be interesting for either party. You will want to know how the office is structured and how design teams operate, the prospects for advancement, and of course before you arrive you will have learned something about the kind of work they do—commercial, residential, or institutional. Certainly, it is not the only interview you have scheduled, nor is this the only firm you are prepared to work for, but interest in the company and eagerness to learn more are always appreciated. Remember that the interviewer wants to

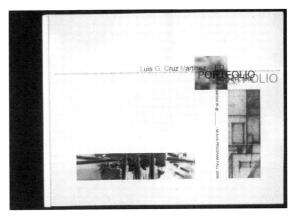

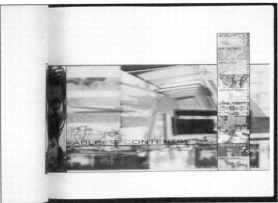

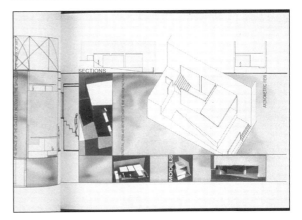

Images from an undergraduate portfolio created in Corel Photo-Paint, designed in Corel Draw, and printed on an HP Deskjet 1120 printer. Luis G. Cruz-Martinez, University of Puerto Rico, San Juan, Puerto Rico. 8 1/2″ x 11″

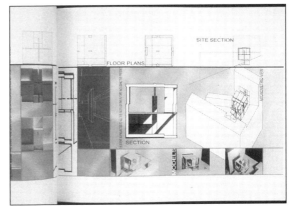

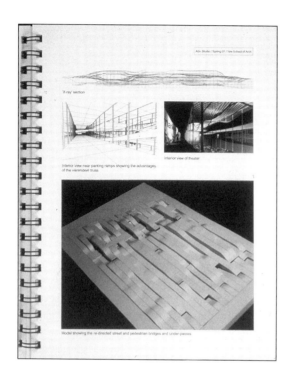

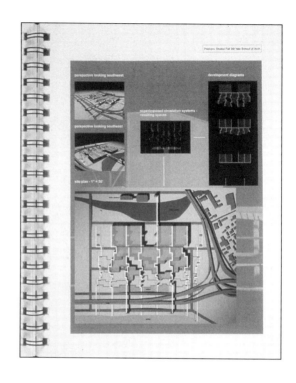

Pages from a graduate portfolio created with
Photoshop, InDesign, and Illustrator, and printed on
an HP Deskjet printer.
Can Tiryaki, Yale University, New Haven, CT.
8 1/2" x 11"

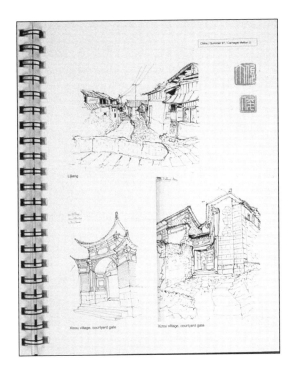

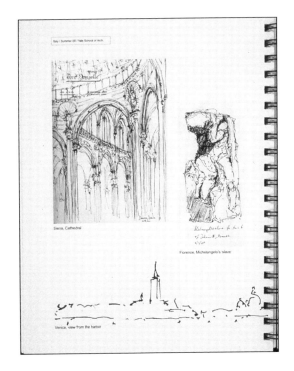

Architectural sketches were arranged to form
an artistic component of the student's portfolio.
Can Tiryaki, Yale University, New Haven, CT.
8 1/2″ x 11″

know what you can do for the company, not what it can do for you. Don't be surprised if someone finds skills in areas of your portfolio and background that result in an offer for employment that you had not planned on, such as graphic designer or web master.

In preparing your portfolio, you must balance two functions. The portfolio is a creative act, showing your skills and imagination, but it is also an act of communication and a tool for self-promotion. Demonstrate originality and inventiveness, but also accept the restrictions and conventions of professionalism, and show that you can get your ideas across in terms that working architects, designers, and graduate faculty can understand. Such a balance between creativity and practicality should come naturally to you. The design of a portfolio may break all the rules, but it must be clear and comprehensible to the viewer by creating its own rules. The struggle between inventiveness and formality is one that will be with you for your entire career as a designer, and the portfolio presentation is where both concepts have to come together naturally, for this is where you tell others what you are capable of doing in your chosen field.

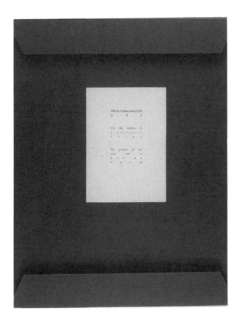

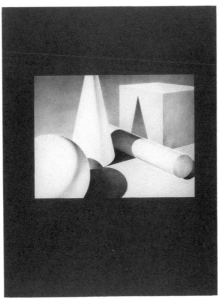
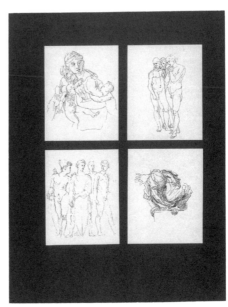

A boxed set of plates in a handmade case of black matte board with a Velcro tab. The type and visuals are carefully arranged and laminated on black boards, with sections clearly demarcated by dividers.

Jillian V. Lustig, Art Center College of Design, Pasadena, CA. 10" x 13"

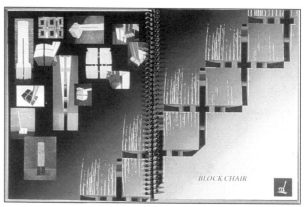

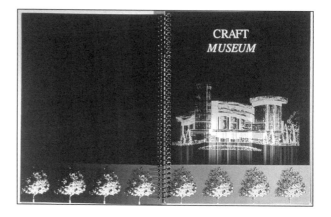

Double-page spreads from an undergraduate portfolio were printed on 11″ x 17″ paper and cut and bound seamlessly into an 8 1/2″ x 11″ portfolio.
Corey Campbell, Lawrence Technological University, Southfield, MI. 8 1/2″ x 11″

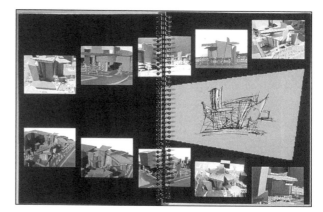

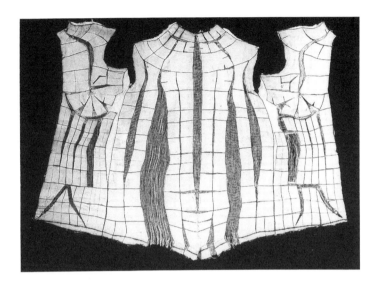

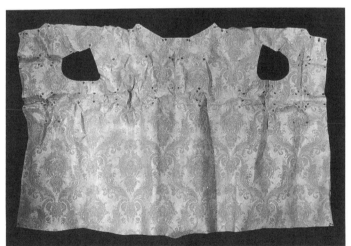

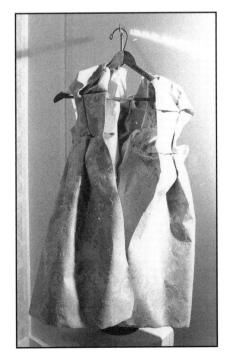

This study in definition of planar surfaces explores the potential of layering and unfolding forms for a graduate thesis project. Through the operation of the fold, a continuous flat surface can be developed into a three-dimensional form integrating the nature of a wall plane with aspects of human form.

Monica Wyatt, Architecture Studio, Cranbrook Academy of Art, Bloomfield Hills, MI. 10″ x 8″

Another portfolio with no explicitly architectural subject matter, this is an exploration of a 1935 Burroughs typewriter to find new forms, meanings, and processes within the component parts. Artistic innovation is evident in the assemblage of resin-coated transparent panels shown in the studio and in photographic prints.

Jonathan Rader, Architecture Studio, Cranbrook Academy of Art, Bloomfield Hills, MI.

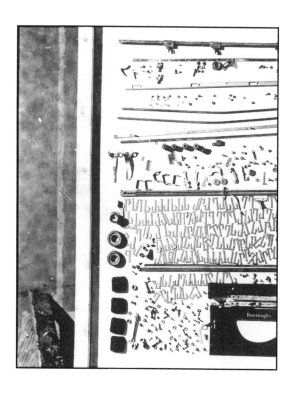

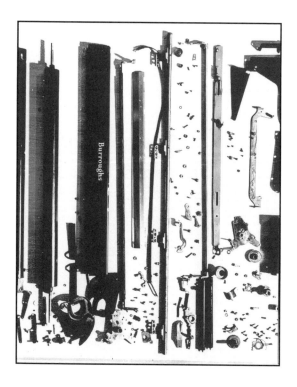

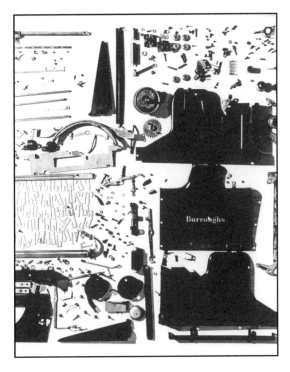

APPENDIX
Workshops

Workshops on portfolio design are simply a
charette, or an opportunity for students to
discover and rehearse an overarching visual
concept for layout design that will guide, contain, animate, and complement all of the key
ingredients of their portfolios. The workshops
I conduct are short-term, lasting perhaps six
to eight hours or, at most, two days. I accompany them with an introductory slide lecture,
discussion of workshop goals, and supplementary materials or handouts. This appendix
includes a summary of some of the guidance I
initiate at workshops as well as samples of
the supplementary materials I provide. It out-
lines the most basic points to consider when

planning a portfolio and therefore helps to jumpstart the organizational process that production of a well-designed portfolio demands.

My slide lecture, which runs about an hour and a half, focuses on the main attributes of graphic design for design portfolios and includes examples and discussion of professionally designed architectural office brochures; the contents and organization of a portfolio; undergraduate, graduate, and post-graduate portfolios (to show strategies for layout); the role of preliminary design drawings and study models; advice on photography, typography, and reproduction methods; tips on handling construction documents and computer-assisted projects; and binder design and materials appropriate to the construction of handmade portfolios. The lecture usually serves to open a dialogue with the students about the contents of the portfolio.

I provide a shopping list of portfolio contents (see below) so students can begin customizing according to their own work and discipline area.

Finally, I ask students to write down a list of all design evidence that will be included in their portfolio and bring the list, with photocopies of their work and appropriate studio materials, to the portfolio workshop that follows, usually on the next day.

Shopping List of Portfolio Contents

- Title page, a simple statement of your name, address, and title of the portfolio

- Design statement, a one-page statement of

your interests, abilities, and direction in design

- Table of contents, a chronological listing of contents with page numbers
- The following photocopies of work:

Photocopies of art/architecture/design studio course work in photocopies; select examples that most accurately reflect the content of your work

Photocopies of construction documents, hand-drafted or in CAD format

Photocopies of computer-aided design, drawing, or animation/video stills, along with an indication of a CD-ROM portfolio package option, if desired

Photocopies of freehand drawing, design drawing, and/or early design experience

Photocopies of elective coursework in related areas of study such as the arts, graphic design, urban planning, or landscape design

- Resume
- Index, to appear at the back of the portfolio, referring to the materials, tools, processes, and special circumstances regarding the creation of your design work

Organizing a Portfolio

Think of organizing a portfolio in the same way you might construct a form such as a building, bridge, or sculpture. Your best work should function as the main supports or fence posts. The number of strong projects you have is a better determinant of your portfolio length than an arbitrary number. The

Cover design and sample pages from the
Master of Architecture thesis presentation of
Matthew Coates, University of Illinois,
Champaign-Urbana, IL. 8 1/2" x 11"

remaining work should serve as the rails that join the supports.

Open the portfolio with a project that is strong and comprehensive, to demonstrate abilities across a broad range of design, including technical and artistic ability. This sets the stage for the rest of your work, which should represent a comprehensive education in design across the spectrum of design coursework and/or office experience. Place another outstanding project in the middle of the portfolio, and close the portfolio with a third strong piece, to demonstrate the consistent quality of work throughout the portfolio and underscore the range of your work.

If you could pick out the three best projects you have, open the portfolio with number one, close the portfolio with number two, and use number three in the middle, life would be easy indeed! Actually, however, there are several strategies for sequencing that take into consideration more complex factors about the work, its reproduction, and how to show a design process. Other factors are orientation (horizontal or vertical), tone (black and white versus color), and any other physical dissimilarities. If the format of your portfolio calls for facing pages, you must consider the juxtaposition of the pieces. If there is no subject theme, work out with your eye what flows best. The basic editing technique is to connect the images in a pleasing and logical pattern.

The first strategy is to begin with simple pieces and finish with complex problems. This simple method has the advantage of

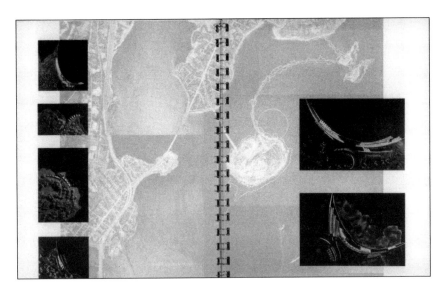

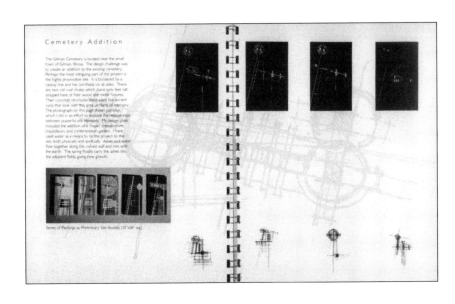

building to a climax—but make sure you actually have the beautiful projects your portfolio is building up to. A portfolio with this strategy might begin with a simple black-and-white sketch problem and lead up to a comprehensive, color, integrated, multi-dimensional campaign with renderings, photographs of study and final models, plan drawings, sections, elevations, and perspectives. Another approach is to think of your portfolio as a musical score. Create a sequence that has a modulated flow built around your strongest pieces. A third strategy is to begin with all your strongest work in a whirlwind of visual excitement and media variations.

Naturally, with any sequencing you must select only strong projects. Do not show anything you feel you need to explain or apologize for. Remember to use and intelligently position your idea sketches. Revealing the process behind important "power" samples adds rich textural experience to your presentation and shows that you know how to think out loud with a pencil, which is of supreme interest to the program to which you are applying or the design management person who is deciding whether to hire you.

Portfolio Suggestions and Reminders

• Portfolios have an average of 20 to 40 sides (a page has two sides, or faces).

• When a resume and cover letter are included, coordinate their design with the portfolio design. The same goes for a business card and envelope.

- Try to design as simple and understated an enclosing system as possible without detracting from the layout and presentation of your work.

- Remember that the underlying invisible grid carries the entire organization throughout the presentation and may even be subtly evidenced in the enclosing system, for instance through the position or orientation of form, shape, and color.

- Rehearse the sequence of projects (that's what the rehearsal portfolio is for) so that you are completely comfortable with their order, subject matter, and relative chronology. Remember to use a sequence strategy based on your best projects and shopping list.

- Title pages for projects can have greater contrast and impact than the rest of the pages, but they should not deviate from the invisible grid that runs throughout the entire portfolio.

- Don't use materials (even in the enclosing system) that are unrelated to anything else in the portfolio.

- Don't use materials that could damage someone's desk.

- All details (page numbers, running heads, titles) should be considered, whether you are doing a plate portfolio or a bound portfolio. Include an index unless it is inappropriate to do so—it allows you to supply all the details about materials, sizes, and courses without cluttering the pages illustrating your work.

- Place your name near the beginning, if not on the cover.

- Craftsmanship is essential in the final product. Cleanliness is also a must.

- At an interview, be prepared to discuss any aspect of your work. You should also research the school or employer. Before going to an interview, have some understanding of the direction of the graduate program and who is on the faculty, or the nature of the company work.

- Relax and enjoy the interview—that's why you have been working so hard and preparing ahead of time.

Suggested Portfolio Design Field Trips (Resources to Explore)

- Photographic house. A full-service photographic house will be able to do copy-stand photography for you and create slides, prints, and perhaps digital images on a disk.

- Presentation house. These are relatively new and are found in the Yellow Pages as computer presentation houses or service bureaus. They can move images from still photographs to disks and burn CD-ROMs. They can also make transparencies from images on disks.

- Paper house. The most comprehensive suppliers of paper products may be found in cities around the country as paper for printers, paper wholesalers, stationers, and art-supply stores.

- Photocopy center. The most well-known

chain of photocopy services in the country is probably Kinko's. Many services and materials are self-evident, but you might want to inquire about color copying, image manipulation, paper products, and binding.

- Bindery. Many cities have full-service book binderies. Look for a smaller operation than a commercial, mass-production, large-volume bindery, which may not have time to work with individual projects.

- Reproduction house. Photostats are one of the easiest and cleanest methods for high-quality line art reproduction where high contrast and size manipulation are important. Typical photostat services include positives, negatives (or reversals), tone or screened image photostats, transparent photostats (cels), mounting services, and more.

- Computer-aided design services. Here, people will help you with projects including graphic design, word processing, and business formats like spread sheets or PowerPoint presentations.

- Video production house. There are companies that specialize in video-production projects, which are typically high-cost and limited in terms of what can be transformed from a still into a video image and vice versa.

SELECTED BIBLIOGRAPHY

Berryman, Greg. *Designing Creative Portfolios.* Menlo Park, California: Crisp, 1994.

———.*Designing Creative Resumes.* Menlo Park, California: Crisp, 1991.

———. *Notes on Graphic Design and Visual Communication.* Los Altos, California: William Kaufmann, 1979.

Biesele, Igildo G. *Graphic Design Education.* New York: Hastings House, 1981.

Brackman, Henrietta. *The Perfect Portfolio.* New York: Watson-Guptill, 1984.

Cohen, Jonathan. *Communication and Design with the Internet.* W. W. Norton, 2000.

Craig, James. *Designing with Type.* New York: Watson-Guptill: 1980.

Foote, Cameron. *The Business Side of Creativity.* New York: W.W. Norton, 1996.

Gray, Bill. Revised by Paul Shaw. *Studio Tips for Artists and Graphic Designers.* New York: W.W. Norton, 1996.

———. *Tips on Type.* New York: W.W. Norton, 1996.

Hofman, Armin. *Graphic Design Manual.* New York: Van Nostrand Reinhold, 1965.

Kliment, Stephen A. *Writing for Design Professionals.* W. W. Norton, 1998.

Marquand, Ed. *How to Prepare Your Portfolio.* New York: Art Direction, 1985.

Metzdorf, Martha. *The Ultimate Portfolio.* Cincinnati: North Light Books, 1991.

Resnick, Elizabeth. *Graphic Design: A Problem-Solving Approach to Visual Communication.* Englewood Cliffs, NJ: Prentice-Hall, 1984.

Scher, Paula. *The Graphic Design Portfolio.* Watson-Guptill, New York, 1992.

White, Jan V. *Graphic Idea Notebook.* New York: Watson-Guptill, 1980.

INDEX

Page numbers in *italics* refer to illustrations.